The Concept of a University

By the same author
The Liberal Mind
Nationalism

The Concept of a University

Kenneth R. Minogue

University of California Press
Berkeley and Los Angeles

University of California Press
Berkeley and Los Angeles, California

© Kenneth R. Minogue 1973

LC 72–95301
ISBN 0–520–02390–0

Printed in Great Britain

Contents

To M.O.

Introduction: Of Heels and Hammers

The theme of this book first appeared at the very dawn of theoretical inquiry, in the famous story about Thales, who fell down a well because he was so busy looking at the stars. Theory and practice, in other words, diverge: whoever genuinely contemplates is unworldly, whilst the vision of the practical man is limited by his ends. Europe's theoretical impulse has largely been cultivated in institutions we refer to either as 'universities' (by virtue of their medieval roots) or as 'academic' (in reference to their Greek inspiration). But with the spread of education in recent times, the original divergence between theory and practice seems to have fallen away. Theory has revealed itself as the secret of power, and vast national resources have been invested in it. This seepage of the practical attitude into the remotest corners of contemplation has greatly increased our present power, but it also limits the range of our imagination. The central concern of the argument that follows, however, is not with what I take to be the long-term intellectual enfeeblement consequent upon this situation, but with the intellectual mistake on which it rests: namely, the assumption that academic inquiry is the same thing as rationality and intellectuality.

There are two obvious reasons why this error has spread. The first is that universities, being educational institutions,

1

are assimilated into our general picture of education in which knowledge is transmitted from teachers with chalk to students with pens. So far as it goes, this picture is adequate enough, but it happens to be peculiarly misleading in the case of universities. It encourages us to construe education as a mechanistic process rather than as an individual adventure; as a result, considerations of efficiency become prominent. In terms of this slightly prosaic manner of thinking, the rather mysterious pre-eminence accorded to universities is commonly found both irritating and baffling. It is often thought to derive from nothing more substantial than social snobbery, and Veblenesque arguments have been deployed in order to reduce the traditional distinction between vocational training and liberal education.

Secondly, the concept of academic inquiry has fallen into obscurity because universities have entered the realm of public discussion. It is of the essence of public discussion that, beginning with some such entity as the state or the nation, it takes the form of fitting whatever it deals with into some larger harmony. The very form of the discussion impels us to regard as fundamental the question: what is the function (or place, role or purpose) of the university? We begin, in other words, by preparing a Procrustean bed for the luckless object of our thought. And the result is that universities are required to fit a variety of functions sponsored by a variety of political and cultural interests: advocacy or prediction has recently taken them to be powerhouses of industrial society, institutions of 'social criticism', promoters of the rate of industrial growth, 'society's response to its troubled sense of something profoundly wrong', and much else.[1]

The habit of seeing the university in functional terms has become so widespread that it can pass itself off as a historical truth. 'If the modern university sees its task as supplying the

---

[1] The first view has been taken by various sociologists, perhaps most notably Daniel Bell; the last is a view taken by F. R. Leavis. See *Nor Shall My Sword*, London 1972.

country with civil servants, administrators and technologists,' runs a typical passage from a modern handbook, 'the medieval university existed to train churchmen, canonists, monks and friars, schoolmen and schoolmasters.' Then, in a further development of this anachronistic discourse, we are told that 'the universities represented . . . the training schools for the established order' and that 'their studies have been more or less closely correlated to the national needs.'[2] What Abelard or Aquinas would have made of an expression such as 'national need' is an interesting speculation. This kind of more or less sociological bias, which reduces universities to featureless and malleable substances reflecting their social context, may appear in impeccably academic studies of the history of education. 'In sociological terms the universities between 1500 and 1600 underwent a change of functions,' writes Professor Kearney. 'They were transformed from being institutions geared to training for a particular profession into institutions which acted as instruments of social control.'[3] Such functional interpretations, which see the university in terms of contingencies irrelevant to its explicit concerns, are inevitably arbitrary and dogmatic.

There is an obvious way in which the understanding of the academic may be liberated from this systematically fruitless addiction to functional treatment. It is to look at what universities do and have done, in an effort to discover what makes them distinctive, quite irrespective of their social context. For to assert that a university is a social institution, part of tertiary education, an instrument of the dominant establishment, a place for teaching the young, or anything similarly generic is to miss the point. Such answers are rather like defining a woman as an unfeathered biped or a rational entity, whereas what one seeks is the uniqueness – what music-hall comedians used to call *la petite différence*. And in following through such an inquiry, we should be prepared

[2] V. H. H. Green, *British Institutions: The Universities*, London 1961, p. 12.
[3] Hugh Kearney, *Scholars and Gentlemen: Universities and Society in Pre-Industrial Britain*, London 1970, p. 30.

to discover that, far from smoothly performing some function within a national system, universities have been almost constantly in a state of conflict with much of the society around them. They have been, so far as public reputation is concerned, almost permanently unsatisfactory institutions. Public discussion has been about little else but reforming them. And if we seek to follow the line of theoretical understanding rather than practical manipulation, we should take such conflict not as an incitement to reform but as a possible clue to the real character of universities.

Indeed, we may regard it as a clue to their essence. And in order to obviate such hostility as may be provoked by the word 'essence', let me hasten to add that there is no question of deducting[4] an *a priori* concept of the university as a timeless entity, but rather of teasing out the features of a historical identity which has been revealing itself, in many varied circumstances, over the last seven or eight centuries. In a quite casual way, we spend a good deal of everyday life in distinguishing essence from function. In a moment of irritation about a confusion of this kind, Hannah Arendt once wrote: 'It is as though I had the right to call the heel of my shoe a hammer because I, like most women, use it to drive nails into the wall.'[5] The kind of distortion imposed upon universities by a functional view may be illustrated by a further analogy. Just as yacht clubs were established by people who just liked 'messing about with boats' (and who had no further end), so universities were established and sustained by people who liked inquiry and scholarly cultivation. Now governments may well regard yacht clubs with approval because they are excellent sources of recruitment for the navy; but it would be absurd to regard this as their function. Similarly, universities have many beneficial side-effects which have sometimes led states to embrace them

[4] Though such an attempt is certainly worthwhile. See 'A Deduction of Universities' by A. Phillips Griffiths, in Reginald D. Archambault (ed.), *Philosophical Analysis and Education*, London 1965.
[5] *Between Past and Future*, London 1961, p. 102.

enthusiastically. But to take any of these side-effects as the function of universities would be a distortion of their character.

The prevalent functional view of universities is part of a general debasement of the very word 'education'. It used to refer to the arrangements by which the young might be brought to the recognition of a certain quality of life, as the result of contact with traditionally recognized forms of study. Among Europeans from medieval times onwards, this meant immersion in the abstract worlds of mathematics and music, in law, and in the literature of Greece and Rome. Such an experience was regarded by some temperaments as valuable for its own sake; nor need it have any very determinate bearing upon what an educated man might do with the rest of his life. No doubt the possession of an education might make some things possible which had not been possible before, but this was a contingency unrelated to the point of education itself. Nor is this situation modified by the fact that many students came to universities, once they were established, with vocational ambitions. This came to be particularly true from that moment in European history, towards the end of the fifteenth century, when the nobility of Europe decided that in order to retain their position as the advisers of kings, they must educate themselves.[6] Such developments as this made it plausible to regard 'education' as 'a preparation for life'. Once this functional view had appeared, it could immediately be inferred that education was dependent upon the kind of life to be expected. It did not take long to become apparent to many thinkers that Greek and Latin are tangential to many conditions of life, and this perception led to an endless succession of possible improvements which would actually correlate what was taught to what was thought to be needed. It is possibly significant to note that these suggestions were generally made by educated men considering what was appropriate to the

---

[6] See: J. H. Hexter, 'The Education of the Aristocracy in the Renaissance', *Journal of Modern History*, vol. XXII, no. 1, March 1950.

lower orders. In time, their work bore fruit in the development, still partially visible today, of two parallel kinds of
pedagogic institution in most European countries. The two
kinds of training may be represented by grammar schools and
universities, on the one hand, which maintained a stubborn
adherence to tradition, and modern or technical schools and
polytechnics, on the other. The latter were explicitly
designed to be concerned with useful knowledge and to be
responsive to changing needs. A mixture of social snobbery
and ideological passion has led to fierce conflicts between the
adherences of one or other of these two traditions, which is a
singular misfortune since there is no reason in principle why
both ought not to be recognized as valuable and necessary.
A clear view of this situation would lead us to distinguish
between the 'socialization' of children, which would include
whatever is necessary in preparing them for later life, and
'education' which is an inculcation of standards of excellence
which are deliberately and inevitably remote from the
parochialities of a child's immediate existence.[7] The relations
between these two things would be complicated, but it
would not be impossible to defend the paradox that one of
the consequences of education in the proper sense is in some
degree to mis-fit a person for the life he is to lead.

To explore the concept of a university requires that we
should present a more or less philosophical argument which
must straddle, rather uneasily, the fields of education and of
social and political theory. It will necessarily be argument in
an impure mode, because much of the discussion with which
we are concerned is itself rhetorical. Further, the material
itself imposes an inescapable indeterminacy upon the conclusions. For modern universities are extraordinarily miscellaneous institutions in which a very large number of
activities are conducted. They thus supply in some degree
evidence that any number of activities might be taken as

[7] Cf. Michael Oakeshott, 'Education: the engagement and its frustration', in
R. F. Dearden, P. H. Hirst and R. S. Peters (eds.), *Education and the Development of
Reason*, London 1972.

central. This is the reason why it is plausible (though, as I shall argue, wrong) to take the view that universities are vital centres of civilization, intellectual powerhouses, areas of 'social criticism' and all the rest. Any attempt to characterize universities in terms of a single criterion will inevitably be wrong. We must consider, amongst other things, the historical circumstances of their foundation, whatever may be inferred from their institutional arrangements, and the kinds of relationship that have appeared between universities on the one hand, and society and culture on the other. We need in particular to be alert to what distinguishes universities from other similar institutions. For the commonest misunderstanding of academic inquiry assimilates it to intellectual uplift, the exercise of rationality, or something else similarly general.

No one who thinks about education for long can remain ignorant of the intimate and ambiguous relation between religious passions and the impulse to theorize. I have devoted a chapter to emphasizing the importance of this relation both to the Greeks who founded schools and to the medieval Christians who founded universities. It seems to me to hold the answer to many curious questions about our intellectual life. For if we look a little below the surface of many modern ideological conflicts about education, such as are discussed in the last section of this book, we shall soon find, beneath the intellectual trappings and the parade of rationality, the unmistakable presence of religious passions.

Part One
The Problem of
Identification

1 The Beginning of Universities

While the details are often obscure, it is clear that the instituting of universities – their 'faint, murky, cloud-wrapped dawn', as Rashdall calls it[1] – was the result of one of those fitful enthusiasms for education which had already several times appeared in the courts of barbaric Europe. Thus Charlemagne had invited the learned Alcuin from England to organize schools in his Frankish realm; and the court of Alfred the Great was in the next century a relatively cultivated place. During this period, in spite of a political and military turmoil which largely yoked men's endeavours to the barest practicalities of life, a collection of cathedral schools came into existence, becoming in time the soil in which universities could grow. In the twelfth century, a collection of intellectual endeavours – editing, collecting, systematizing – culminated in bands of scholars setting up *studia generalia*. These were places of learning which, by virtue of the fame of their teachers, could attract students from all over Christendom: it was precisely this universal significance which made such *studia* also *generalia*. The two centres which became by virtue of their considerable distinction the models of later foundations were Paris and

[1] Hastings Rashdall, *The Universities of Europe in the Middle Ages*, ed. F. M. Powicke and B. Emden, Oxford 1936.

Bologna; but they were rapidly succeeded by many other centres, so that a network of such institutions soon stretched in Europe from Spain at one end to Poland and Bohemia at the other. In Paris the scholars, and in Bologna the students, found it advantageous to band together into a legal corporation, and consequently acquired the term *universitas*, a term which might be used of any kind of legal association; towards the end of the Middle Ages it was coming to be restricted to what we now call universities. This organizational character of universities is in a number of respects just as important as their intellectual distinction, for it is here that we may find the secret of that astonishing longevity, that capacity for decay and revival which has marked the university out as distinct from any of the other scholarly institutions of other times and other civilizations. Universities were, as Rashdall puts it, 'products of that instinct of association which swept like a great wave over the towns of Europe in the course of the eleventh and twelfth centuries'. And for several centuries, until political sovereignty began to impair their independence, they exercised the corporate freedom of feudalism to the full.

Spontaneity soon gave place to artifice: in 1224 (by which time many other universities, including Oxford, were well established) Frederick II founded a *studium generale* in Naples, and in 1229 Pope Gregory IX did the same at Toulouse. The intention of each of these eminent founders was that the new creations should be the equals in prestige of Paris and Bologna; and in an attempt to achieve by decree what is really only susceptible to voluntary acquiescence, a Papal bull of 1233 asserted that anyone admitted to mastership at Toulouse should be allowed to teach in any other *studium* without further examination. The bull did not meet with universal acceptance, and the more successful *studia* were always suspicious of the prerogatives of other universities. Nonetheless, the granting of the *ius ubique docendi* came to be the distinguishing mark of universities; and founding them was recognized as the prerogative of imperial or ecclesiastical authority. By this time, their intellectual eminence gave them an important role in the life of European Christendom. Intellectually able young men of all ranks of society flocked to study at them, and many such graduates, after studying, came to occupy influential positions in the Church and the administration of realms. There were even occasions when medieval writers placed *Studium* as a co-ordinate power in medieval society alongside the powers of Church (*Sacerdotium*) and State (*Regnum*). Something new and valuable had arisen in the feudal firmament.

Love of learning may best be seen as but a part of a wider movement of dissatisfaction with current things which led to new styles of architecture, to a new strictness in monastic disciplines, to a reformation of the Church and to all the other manifold currents which make up what historians have come to call the twelfth-century renaissance. A time of great dissatisfaction with contemporary standards took an intellectual direction. Further, there is in sociological terms no adequate explanation for this turn of events.[2] Europe was indeed slightly more prosperous in the eleventh century than she had been previously; and the indiscriminate raiding of the Northmen had at last ceased. Peace may marginally have helped the movement along; but its roots run back with little break for some centuries. This new movement is attributable to the logically unpredictable human capacity for looking upon situations afresh, a part – but only a part – of which has been captured in Professor Knowles's organic image of the period as 'Europe's adolescent awakening'.

What kind of intellectual dissatisfaction led to this educational creativity? Christian belief and legal practice – the two most conspicuous areas of revival – had long been left to the play of imagination and practicality. But imagination is tolerant of contradictions – indeed, as in the *credo quia impossibile*, it may welcome them; and practice builds

---

[2] The decisive reason is logical: there can be no *general* explanation of the uniqueness of an event.

up, over time and in response to the enormous variety of particular circumstances, a chaotic jumble of expedient rules. Men of an intellectual bent find both situations unsatisfactory. It happened that early in the eleventh century, Roman Law, as it had been systematized under Justinian, became available to a number of scholars in Italy, and supplied a dazzling model of intellectual coherence with which the practices of the European communities – varying admixtures of customary law with debased fragments of remembered Roman practice – might be compared. After the revival of the study of Roman Law, associated with the name of Irnerius, came the standardization of canon law by Gratian. The very title of his famous textbook – the *Concord of Discordant Canons* – clearly indicates its character. This was the most famous of those books which defined issues and laid out the conflicting statements of authorities and principles; and sometimes, indeed, went on to provide a resolution of the issue. It was not, however, the first enterprise of this kind; nor was the enterprise limited to law. Similar projects were already being pursued in theology. This is, of course, a work of practical value, and it was recognized as such by the students who were soon flocking to Bologna, and later to Padua and the other schools of law which arose. But to see it as a practical enterprise is to miss what gave this passion its enormous capacity for creating institutions and shaping minds: the love of dialectic, the search for truth, the spirit summed up in one of the many meanings of St Anselm's formula *credo ut intelligam*. Further, this enthusiasm for knowledge might and did spring up in any of the ranks of feudal society. The sparse records reveal such men as the Picard nobleman Baldwin II, Count of Guines (Bloch describes him as 'hunter, toper and great wencher'), who arranged to have translated for him Aristotle's *Physics* and the *Geography* of the Roman grammarian Solinus. But the pre-eminent example of such a spirit was, of course, Peter Abelard, who deserted the knightly vocation his circumstances suggested in order to carve out for himself a new life in the sphere of learning. Abelard's *Sic et Non* was the classical expression of contemporary dialectic. A millennium of Christian thought, far from having rendered the faith coherent, had left unresolved a great number of disputed questions: that, in the Trinity, each is one with the other had been both affirmed and denied in the writings of the Fathers; and questions such as whether the Angels had been created before Heaven and Earth, whether Joseph had suspected Mary of adultery and whether it is permitted to kill men or not, could all be answered authoritatively in different senses. To describe the activity of elucidating questions like these, Abelard adapted the term *theologia* by which it is still known. Some of these questions appear, at a distance of eight centuries, to be somewhat less pressing than they were to Abelard; but others (that of pacifism, for example) are perennially disputable.

The prestige of universities in the Middle Ages was enormous, and it rested upon an admiration for 'education' – an admiration which, in our present age of universal literacy, is difficult to recapture. Medieval men seem to have thought of universities in the way an improverished craftsman regards the brilliant child for whose education he is making sacrifices; and they bequeathed support to universities with the same open generosity with which they endowed the huge Gothic cathedrals of Europe. At the lowest level, no doubt, they were impressed by the mystery of wisdom contained in books; for to illiterates every book has the romance of secrecy. More impressive still, these books were written in a language remote from everyday life; to learn it was to acquire the capacity of living in the remote classical world, never forgotten, always valued. Above all, the universities were the beneficiaries of the persistent dualism of medieval Christian thought: men lived in two worlds, one here and now, a world of material things in which life was constant toil and ceaseless scheming to provide the necessities and distractions of life; the other world, of which the Church was the custodian, was spiritual and superior to anything directly known on earth. Here were Augustines' two cities, and human beings lived at the point of intersection between them. At death a man might hope to promote himself from the one to the other; but a special reverence was given to men who, so far as it was humanly possible, already lived exclusively for (and to some extent within) this other world. They wanted priests to be visibly distinct from other men; and particularly after the Lateran Council of 1215 this tradition was sharply enforced. It is easily understandable that medieval men should have sought to understand the distinctiveness of the don in these easily available religious terms. 'For,' as an edict of the University of Oxford, obliging tailors to cut academic dress to ample proportions, said in 1358, 'it is decent and reasonable that those whom God has distinguished with inner qualities from laymen also be different from laymen in appearance.' A concern with books and learning had, indeed, begun centuries before in the shelter of the cloisters; and a vocation to be a clerk seemed no very mysterious thing to a community accustomed to priests, monks and nuns. As a result of these beliefs, the members of a university lived generally under another jurisdiction from that of the townspeople among whom, and often in deadly enmity with whom, they resided. In Oxford, in Paris, in Bologna, the populations detested students for their turbulence as much as they admired universities for the economic benefits they brought and the mysterious realm they were thought to inhabit. It was a time in which anti-clericalism and religiosity could run easily together: universities became involved in both feelings.

The philosophical paradigm of the academic world is to be found in the dialogues of Plato. What we commonly find there is Socrates beginning an inquiry in the market place, an inquiry that soon reveals the answers of the market place to be confused. In the developed doctrine of the forms, practical life is characterized by opinion, which sometimes corresponds to the truth and sometimes does not, and the business of the philosopher is to move – the metaphor is usually one of ascent – by the use of reasoning to a form of understanding which may appropriately be called knowledge. Knowledge is an understanding of the principle of things, and is composed of clear ideas or forms from which the accidental and contingent associations inevitably found in the world have been purged. As an account of the two realms – 'the world' or 'practice' on the one hand and 'philosophy' on the other – this Platonic distinction remains a structure on which a large number of interesting variations may be performed. But in the early centuries of the Christian era it was inevitably overtaken by theological preoccupations, and pressed into service as a scaffolding for Christian theology. For no one could fail to recognize the similarity between the philosopher who by reasoning 'left the world behind' and the hermit, monk or anchorite who abandoned 'the world' and devoted himself so far as was humanly possible to the service of Christ. When the universities were founded, an enthusiasm for piety and an enthusiasm for learning were not easily to be distinguished. Since the academic used reason, and since Reason was also the mode of God's creation, the academic could be thought of as inhabiting a world whose remoteness was similar to that of the monk or the mystic: and similarly closer to God. Philosophy might well be seen – it was by John of Salisbury – as a Jacob's ladder linking the clerk to heaven; linking him indeed more effectively than simple faith might manage, for (as J. Bass Mullinger has put it) 'a belief sprang up that an intelligent apprehension of spiritual truth depended on a current use of prescribed methods of argumentation.'[3] Thus Hugh of St Victor, early in the twelfth century, can approve as definitions of philosophy both that it is 'a meditation about death' (and therefore a mental attitude that above all is suited to Christians who live in anticipation of a heavenly future) and that it is 'a discipline that investigates the probable causes of all things human and divine'.

Even in the Middle Ages it soon became clear that the

[3] *Encyclopaedia Britannica*, 9th ed., 1883.

17

academic world need not be identified with the other-world-liness of the Christian. The very method of dialectic – which began with an assembly of arguments and authorities tending to contradictory conclusions – would immediately suggest that reason was a two-edged weapon which might as easily destroy as reinforce faith. Those whom reason led from the path of orthodoxy generally went on this journey inadvertently, for it required no very severe discipline to keep in one fold men who had no desire to stray. Among the few heretical beliefs proscribed in the University of Oxford in the thirteenth century, proposals for the simplification of Latin grammar have as prominent a place as actual heresies. Still, learning was very early recognized as a potential source of the sin of pride. One master 'declared that he understood the Pauline Epistles better than St Paul himself, [and] lost all his learning forthwith, until a girl was appointed as his tutor who with difficulty succeeded in teaching him the seven penitential psalms',[4] and Robert de Sorbon warned that 'clerks busy themselves with eclipses of the sun, but fail to observe the darkening of their own hearts by sin.'[5]

The danger that the 'other world' of the universities might not coincide with that of Christianity led in the sermons of the time to a collection of exemplary tales of professors whose conceit of dialectical skill was divinely punished. It was the achievement of the high century of Scholasticism to produce a synthesis – in the strict technical sense – of faith and reason; the generation of Aquinas composed a world in which all the cognitive faculties united to generate a single image of the creation, both that which is visible and that which is not. And when, in the next century, this image began to dissolve again into discordant fragments, the theory of double truth, borrowed from Averroes, was available to allow the universities a certain amount of freedom in which to roam without denying the propositions of the faith. For

[4] C. H. Haskins, *The Rise of Universities*, New York 1923, p. 75.
[5] C. H. Haskins, *Studies in Mediaeval Culture*, Oxford 1929, pp. 49–51.
Cf. Rashdall, *op. cit.*, vol. i, pp. 454–5.

academically speaking the experience of the mystic, the writings of the Fathers and the theological assumptions of Churchmen might all feature as objects of inquiry and criticism; all of these things belonged, in an important sense, to a practice of life from which the university was in principle remote. If this is realized, then the ivory tower of the academic can no longer be assimilated to the other world of the Christian. It then becomes necessary to specify the academic world in other terms; possibly in the procedures by which it seeks objectivity.

Being seen as an institution with roots in another world, the university did not recruit its members by birth, but rather by vocation. They came from all ranks of feudal society, so that the student with his own servant jostled his impoverished fellow who lived merely on tripe and the cheapest kinds of sausage. The giving of alms was a medieval duty; and the poor scholar qualified as a recipient of them. Universities soon established 'poor chests' which served as provision for the scholar without resources of his own. This diversity of social origin was combined with an equal variation in countries of origin, so that most of the major continental universities were organized in 'nations' of students, subordinate corporations within a university which was in all senses a world apart from the intense localism of the cities, and even more, of the feudal countryside. During the first few centuries of their existence, universities constituted an entirely 'international' society in which men might move with entire freedom, being marked neither in their actions nor in their writings by any very evident national or regional individuality. As the Middle Ages gave way to what by convention are recognized as modern times, this international character came to be contested by patriotic devotion to sovereign and realm: a political influence which long afterwards reached its apex of exclusiveness in nineteenth-century nationalism. But it has been one of the peculiar strengths of universities to have developed a set of attitudes, standards and conventions which resisted parochialism. Such universality is an important part of civilization; and once, under the wing of the Church, it emerged from the parochialism of the barbarians, it was tenacious. Universities never lost for long their remoteness from the divisive allegiances of practical life. While many ambitious men sought to pursue their careers in the universities, and while in day-to-day living both students and masters shared the ordinary human preoccupations, universities were always concerned with matters at a tangent from the confined circles of practicality. What they provided was, in form, the kind of training which might turn a man into the same sort of scholar as his teachers. Most of the students of medieval universities, of course, had no ambition to devote their lives to academic pursuits. Once any institution has been successfully established, it will be seen as a source of profit and advancement. Men studied, graduated, and then, as educated men, went out into the world to seek their fortune in whatever way circumstances and their own wits might suggest.

It might seem from this account that the distinctive feature of medieval universities was their revolt against accepted ideas. Their history might be told in such a way as to confirm the popular current view of originality as a consequence of rebellion. Abelard's career easily fits this stereotype. His well-known account of one of his teachers, Anselm of Laon, tells us a good deal about his own impatient spirit: 'a wonderful flow of words he had, but their sense was despicable and empty of all rational argument. When he lit a fire, he filled his house with smoke; no illumination came.' What dissatisfied Abelard was that his predecessors had merely been collectors; the prickly mind of Abelard saw problems everywhere, and he attained a vast popularity among students by exhibiting the Christian faith as a dark continent, to be mapped and comprehended by the new kind of dialectical inquiry. His work was a kind of agenda and was in one direction very quickly completed in the *Sentences* of Peter the Lombard, who produced a textbook which remained in active currency for five hundred years and which already exhibits the Scholastic method which was brought to perfection in the next century by men like Aquinas.

Abelard's account of himself as a rebel is a legend which has these days the disadvantage of being fashionable; it needs immediately to be corrected by the reminder that the rise of universities was just as fundamentally a renaissance, and depended upon a vigorous and dedicated re-entry into a heritage which had been lying around more or less unused for many generations, its mere external forms preserved in the depths of the monasteries. One might well say of classical culture during the barbarian period what Maitland said of the *Digest of Roman Law*: 'it barely escaped with its life.' But the more the intellectual life of the eleventh and twelfth centuries has been studied, the more it has been seen to depend upon survivals from the ancient world. The metaphor of rekindling embers is hard to avoid: as Rashdall says of the medical school at Salerno: 'The smouldering sparks of scientific culture which had survived from the old-world illumination were fanned into a flame by the first breath of that mysterious new spirit which at this time began to move upon the face of European civilization.'[6] A small but crucial selection of classical texts and manuals – more or less accidental survivals in the desolation – were the indispensable conditions of what was achieved. In the memorials of the time, William of Conches is remembered for his striking recognition of this fact: 'We are dwarfs, but we stand upon the shoulders of giants.' The consequent respect for books and authorities became in time the characteristic vice of Scholasticism. Education came to be merely the transfer of propositions from books to the mind; and the custodians of universities found their distinctiveness in the contrast between books on the one hand and the visible universe on the other – a corruption fittingly attacked in Bacon's preference for things over words. The modern world lives largely

[6] Rashdall, *op. cit.*, vol. 1, p. 78.

in the shadow of its rejection of a mechanical scholasticism –
a spirit not the less powerful amongst those who have merely
learned it scholastically from books and schoolmasters. It
is a spirit which has made us value intelligence and originality far more than memory, which we often regard merely as
a mechanical faculty of storage and recall, fit only for the
machines. This disposition has meant that in interpreting
moments of great cultural intensity we attend more happily
to what we can interpret as revolt than to what we must
interpret as submission to authority. But even a cursory
inspection of the twelfth-century renaissance will make us
aware that its achievements rested also upon a humble capacity to understand that the inherited texts did contain things
of great value and to build an academic structure upon the
business of eliciting them. Hence it is crudely possible to
interpret this period either as rebellion against authority or
as submission to authority; but an examination which rises
beyond these facile shibboleths will recognize that both the
submission and the rebellion are carelessly apprehended
parts of a complicated set of events.

The rise of the universities belongs to a class of cultural
moments in which a generation's dissatisfaction with the state
of its intellectual inheritance led to a range of new achievements. There are not many such moments. Perhaps the most
celebrated of them is the birth of 'science' among the Ionian
Greeks of the sixth century BC. In the succeeding two or
three centuries, Greek speculation produced a body of work
which has been the substance of rationality ever since. One
episode within this experience has become so celebrated as
to stand as an image of this kind of moment: namely,
Socrates' dissatisfaction with the moral and political notions
he found circulating in the *agorai* of Greek states. It was
Socrates' pupil Plato who founded in the groves of Academe
a school which in some respects and for some purposes might
be counted as the first university. This entire experience is
endlessly praised in accounts of the Western heritage. There
is another moment which has a similar celebrity: the

multiplicity of intellectual events from about 1450 to 1700 to which the labels of Renaissance and Scientific Revolution are often attached. The rise of the universities was a cultural moment of comparable importance, yet the curious fact is that it has generally failed to elicit the same enthusiasm from the custodians of our intellectual past. To understand why is to discover a good deal about the sea of attitudes which wash around the walls of today's universities.

Part of the reason, no doubt, is that the very words 'feudal' and 'medieval' operate in the twentieth century as terms of abuse. The modern world has identified itself very largely in terms of what it rejected from its predecessor, something revealed even by the very title it gave that predecessor: the 'Middle' Ages. It chose to regard this period as an unprofitable interlude between its own excellence and the ancient fountainhead of rationality. Fathers cannot compete with grandfathers in popularity. For very complicated reasons – some religious, some cultural – we have inherited from the philosophers of the Enlightenment a prejudice which sees the period from Charlemagne to Charles v as a barely qualified darkness.[7] As a consequence modern liberals have chosen to attribute the representative institutions they admire rather to the Athenian *demos* than to the medieval Parliament; constitutional liberties have been attributed to nationalist pamphleteers in order to avoid the unwelcome discovery that their main source lies in the legal practices of a divided Christendom, and the essence of universities has been found in the classical spirit of rationality rather than in the medieval

[7] This caricature is particularly common in educational writings. Thus within a few pages of a typical case we may read: 'With the end of the Roman Empire in the fifth century, a curtain of darkness descended over Europe. . . . The bright light surrounding the School of Charlemagne in the eighth century faded . . . darkness descended once more, but the darkness was not as deep as formerly. Though little was added, in these years, to the sum of knowledge, the old was not entirely lost, so that when, four centuries later, the light began to return, the foundations on which the revival of learning might be were still there.' Elizabeth Lawrence, *The Origins and Growth of Modern Education*, London 1970, pp. 52–5. The ritual element of this electric metaphor indicates the scholastic character of this view of scholasticism.

spirit of corporate association, which itself depends upon a Christian conception of individuality. The eccentric thing about this strange prejudice is that liberals fighting against the extremely common modern impulse towards despotism have often owed their victories to a cultural plurality inherited from the Middle Ages.

There is another obvious reason why the medieval beginnings of universities have not commanded vast respect. Those who do not understand either the character or the value of universities are inclined to treat them as technological powerhouses; and the importance of universities will, consequently, be judged in terms of their contribution to science and, particularly, technology. Seen in these terms, the medieval university has often been judged as a failure; the cultivation of physics, which was part, though only a part, of the intellectual activity of medieval universities, has been ignored in favour of a few jibes about angels dancing on the point of a needle. Seen through this distorting screen, the history of universities in the first few centuries hops from Roger Bacon in Oxford to Galileo at Padua, and hastens on to the second half of the seventeenth century when Newton and Locke appear. Only then, and only very imperfectly, did universities appear as suppliers of stimulating technical ideas to the rest of society; so that intellectual history written in these terms has an unavoidably carping tone until it arrives in the nineteenth century.

This view of universities is part of the modern world's attempt to free itself and establish an independent identity. But it is also part of an important and influential doctrine about human destiny which in theological, moral and political forms dates back to the sixteenth century. Here is Hobbes' mid-seventeenth-century version, clearly an ancestor of the functional view of universities we have discussed in the previous section:

That which is now called an *University*, is a joining together, and an incorporation under one government, of many public schools, in one and the same town or city. In which the principal schools were ordained for the three professions, that is to say, of the Roman religion, of the Roman law, and of the art of medicine. And for the study of philosophy it hath no otherwise place, than as a handmaid to the Roman Religion: and since the authority of Aristotle is only current there, that study is not properly philosophy (the nature whereof dependeth not on authors), but *Aristotelity*. And for geometry, till of very late times, it had no place at all; as being subservient to nothing but rigid truth. And if any man by the ingenuity of his own nature, had attained to any degree of perfection therein, he was commonly thought a magician, and his art diabolical.[8]

Hobbes had spent a part of his early life as secretary to Francis Bacon, and while the two men disagreed upon a great number of things they did share an attitude to education and to universities. They belonged to a generation of men greatly excited by technological advance. Each of them thought in terms of a politically sovereign realm which might be organized to produce and generate new technological discoveries. Bacon particularly thought of men in terms reminiscent of the book of Genesis, as the custodians of a vast garden which could be made to yield vastly greater quantities of 'fruit'.[9] Until the beginning of the seventeenth century the political resources for making a society of this character did not exist; but from the time when the idea of political sovereignty had become current, the state was always available as a powerful organizing agency which might (and often did) use its organization in the service of production. Enlightened government in the eighteenth century, and projects of central planning of the economy in the nineteenth and twentieth, are more highly developed versions of the same doctrine.

Now it is clear that universities could provoke little but hostility from this tradition of thought. When Leibnitz

[8] Thomas Hobbes, *Leviathan*, ed. Michael Oakeshott, Oxford, ch. 46. Cf. ch. 30, p. 225.
[9] See particularly *The New Atlantis*.

B

25

attacked the universities for 'monkish erudition' he struck with each word at precisely what was thought most objection-able in them. Whereas the Middle Ages had valued universities because of their distance from the world and its endeavours, now modern men began to object that univers-ities were in need of reform for exactly the opposite reason: because they did not contribute to what was seen as a cooperative endeavour from which no individual or institu-tion might be allowed exemption: contributing to national wealth and power. The proper solution to these conflicts was found in the seventeenth and later centuries by the creation of large numbers of Academies of Arts and Science, Trade Schools, Seminaries, Technical Institutes, Polytechnics, etc. All of these catered to the diffusion of useful knowledge. It is obvious that this technological tradition has determined a great deal of the world we live in; and it is very difficult not to welcome some of its consequences and regret others. Different people will make different judgements on this matter. The creation and use of technology must be seen as one entirely legitimate social activity among others. But like many other social activities, a passion for technology has a tendency to become so excited by its own possibilities as to become blind to all else. The clearest example of this kind of blindness is perhaps the Saint-Simonian religion of produc-tivity, but there are few important modern movements which have not absorbed one or other element of it.

Universities, then, have no place in this scheme; they are not devoted to the improvement of the world, and their attention is focused upon intellectual and historical realms remote from the urgencies moving men in day-to-day endeavour. They have, therefore, often been found infuriat-ingly unresponsive to what have seemed to many to be the obvious and overriding needs of mankind. But remote as they are, universities have not been so entirely remote as to discourage entirely the hope that they might be subdued. They have been interpreted as rather inefficient institutions for transmitting skill; and the believer in a single world of producers has been able to stand forward not as a clear enemy of universities, bent on destryoying them, but simply as a reformer, who would correct what every reasonable man must recognize as their deficiencies. This kind of attack has obviously found its most receptive audience at times when universities have been in a decadent condition. At the beginning of modern times, for example, it seems to have been true that many universities had fallen into such a mechanical respect for the authority of existing sources that they failed to provoke much response from many enthusiastic and intelligent men. But in all such cases of decadence, universities have managed to rouse themselves and to supply the necessary recovery of vitality from within. Indeed, it seems likely that the effort of fighting off alien projects of reform has itself served to kindle that very necessary vitality.

It seems clear, then, that from the seventeenth century to the twentieth, there has been a continuous tradition of attack on universities which takes the form of regretting their isolation from the world, and which despises their 'monkish erudition'. This tradition stretches from Leibnitz's desire that universities should become centres where 'savants and students should participate as much as they can with other people and in the world' to the twentieth-century demands (from groups as disparate as student militants on the one side, and businessmen on the other) that universities should become more 'relevant' to the present time. It does not affect the matter that each group and each generation has happened to have its own parochial notion of 'relevance'; nor need we limit our account of these hostilities to the seventeenth century. As far back as 1381 the citizens of Cambridge burst into the common chest of the university and made a bonfire of many university documents. A lady named Margaret Storre is said to have taken particular pleasure in casting the incinerated documents to the winds, crying: 'Away with clerical learning, away with it.'[10] Her exact

[10] M. B. Hackett, *The Original Statutes of Cambridge University*, Cambridge 1970, p. 3.

motives are obscure, but she may stand as one of the earliest (and least intellectual) of the university's critics.

We are now in a position to recognize that the functionalist view of universities – that their studies have always 'been more or less closely correlated to the national needs' – is not a historical generalization but the covert appearance of a political doctrine about universities, a doctrine which arises from a view of society as a single field of endeavour within which all activities are more or less 'contributory'. The insinuation of such a doctrine as a historical truth prepares the way for its emergence in other contexts as a criterion of change. For if universities always *have* contributed, why should they not contribute more efficiently? But it is with institutions as with people: we rightly admire those who preserve a valuable identity by responding to new circumstances but we despise those people who shift and change with every passing wind of fashion. Adaptability is admirable, instability despicable; but how shall we tell the difference between them? Neither persons nor institutions can steer a proper course in the face of diverging influences unless they have a firm grasp on their own identity. In universities this identity may be found on the one hand in its organization and on the other in the special character of its intellectual preoccupations.

These two elements of identity are quite unambiguous. 'Education' has from early times referred to a special manner of inculcating a very particular heritage derived from the classical world. All wider meanings are extensions of that core, and since the word has a nice sound (whereas neighbouring terms like 'persuasion' and 'propaganda' and 'training' are all dubious in various ways) it has been very widely extended. So far as the meaning of 'education' is concerned, we need not distinguish between schools and universities. Both involve a classroom encounter between teacher and pupil on the basis of a body of knowledge which must be more than merely useful. In recent times, however, strenuous efforts have been made to break down any distinction between the classroom and the world outside; and in pursuance of this objective such disparate activities as canoeing through rapids, emptying dustbins, sitting on the ground in circles seeking 'personal communion', and living for a fixed period on Indian reservations in America have all been practised as education. Such changes in what people do in schools and at universities have been supported by the proposition that learning – which is, of course, a much wider human propensity than education – ought not to be confined to the classroom. Since no one seems ever to have supposed the contrary, however, this reasoning makes the whole matter more, rather than less, mysterious. Part of the mystery disappears when we remember that the classroom has commonly been regarded as a place of misery. Everyone has crept unwillingly and snail-like to school; and everybody has had his Huckleberry Finn moments when the desk is a prison, the teacher's voice drones boringly on, and outside the woods and streams, perhaps even the dustcart and the Indian reservations, call seductively. The new modes of education can at least present themselves as a liberation from drudgery; and any increase in the world's pleasure may legitimately be welcomed. Yet it is surely strange to believe that so many generations so pointlessly immured themselves in schoolrooms to no purpose.

And indeed, a moment's thought will show that they did not do so. For education appears in European history as an object of love, and while there were no doubt unwilling pupils many in fact sought out an education and chose to live out their lives in academic circumstances. These were times when schooling was a matter of choice. But when education (in which only a few are interested) came to be confused with useful knowledge (in which everyone must be concerned) a new situation arose. All children were now sent off to schools which taught a somewhat pragmatic compromise between useful knowledge and education. By and large, the academic element in education managed to survive only at the cost of imposing a good deal of pointless drudgery on the majority

29

of pupils. It is this majority who are prominent among those understandably attracted by the project of breaking down the barriers between life and school. But such is the current confusion of thought that many imagine that the breaking down of these barriers is an improvement in education, rather than a destruction of it. They seek the abolition of the academic for they see it in functional terms, as no more than a barrier (generally stigmatized as one of privilege) dividing society into different parts. But this raises issues about the relation between the university and outside opinion, issues which we shall postpone to Part Three.

2 Religion and Academic Freedom

We need consider nothing more elaborate than the sketch of academic beginnings already provided in order to realize that universities first grew in religious soil. For it was the Christian religion which first supplied the institutional opportunity of a recognized class of men whose temperament was thought to have removed them from the world. No monks, no universities; for as Rashdall has remarked: 'In the age which preceded the rise of the universities, the monks were the great educators of Europe.'[1] The educational activities of the early monks were merely incidental to their devotions; but by the thirteenth century we may find in the Franciscans and Dominicans teaching orders which had made education a direct and primary interest. It is this close connection with religion which has made some modern commentators, whose hostility to Christianity obscures their understanding of religious phenomena, prefer ancient Greece as the hearth of the flame of rationality. It is possible to present the Greek experience as rationality flaring out of the darkness of more primitive beliefs: possible, but unwise. For even a very superficial second look[2] will convince us that

[1] Rashdall, *op. cit.*, vol. i, p. 344.
[2] F. M. Cornford has provided something much more than a superficial look: see *From Religion to Philosophy*, London 1912.

philosophy and science were but the children of religious preoccupations, and that they only occasionally and casually managed a temporary independence. It is but an anachronistic legend to present the pre-Socratics as rationalists struggling against superstition, or to forget the *daimon* of Socrates in order to present him as a kind of Victorian agnostic freethinker.

For these reasons, their religious parentage is the dark side of our understanding of universities, and it is not hard to see why. Religious authorities have often persecuted intellectual men, and Abelard, Roger Bacon, Bruno and Galileo are but the first names that come to mind in a series of celebrated martyrdoms. The details are often complicated, and sometimes the history belies the legend. But whatever the qualifications, there are serious reasons for thinking that there is, in the nature of things, a fundamental conflict between religion on the one hand and the search for truth on the other. Common opinion sees religion as hostile to science; and similar episodes could be cited in philosophy and literature. Now although this view rests upon a number of misapprehensions, it is not entirely false. And if it is in any sense true that there must be conflict between religion and the universities, then we would seem to be faced with something close to a paradox: although religion inspires the pursuit of truth, it also constricts it, and academic freedom becomes a demand asserted against religion. These questions impel us to seek a clear notion of religion.

The common view is that religion is the option of believing in God. Believers are religious, non-believers are not. This is a serious mistake, because it takes certain parochial emphases in Christianity to be the essence of the matter. For the proposition that God exists, or even a belief in a variety of gods, is clearly not so much religion itself as a possible, and indeed common, conclusion arrived at by many religions. To evade this pressure of the parochial upon us, we should do better to go back before Christianity to the Romans who bequeathed us the word. *Religio* meant something that binds together, and the Roman religion consisted fundamentally in a sense of membership of the providential community of the *populus Romanus*. A good deal followed from this, of course. The Romans believed in a pantheon of gods, and saw it as their duty to build suitable houses for these gods to inhabit. The gods were powerful, and if treated properly, helpful. But they required that rituals should be performed and a priestly class grew up to conduct these rituals. The gods spoke, furthermore, in a special language which had to be professionally interpreted: they spoke by signs – by auguries signified in the flight of birds across the sky, or in the condition of the liver of the sacred geese. A further part of the Roman religion was a belief in the wisdom and sanctity of ancestors and, above all, the presiding ancestor of the Roman people, Romulus. This cult of the ancestral had important political consequences for Roman politics: the authority of the Senate, for example, derived from its association with the Roman past.

Every religion, of course, has its own peculiarities, and these are likely to mislead us. The advantage in taking the Romans as an example is partly a matter of their remoteness from us, and partly a matter of the contrast between their religion and that of Christians. For one thing, the Roman religion was hardly at all a matter of choice: men were either born Romans or they were not. This situation changed in the later Republic, and was transformed under the Empire as the right of citizenship was extended, especially by Caracalla; nor indeed were the Romans ever as exclusive as the Greek states about whom they would admit to citizenship. Nevertheless we do not find the question of choice intruding on religion as it does in the case of Christianity. For another thing, the Romans seem to have had very little interest in theology and they took the question of belief lightly. Like most peoples of the ancient world they were relatively tolerant of other people's religions and perfectly prepared to modify their practices and to recognize the deities of other peoples as real. Finally the Roman religion is typical of most

33

in that it is essentially based upon an existing community, and therefore no gap opens up between the political and the spiritual. Such a gap is exactly what made Christianity so different a religion from its competitors.

We may describe a religion as the practices by which a group of people assert the coherence of their lives. The central idea of religion is the notion of a whole whose parts are the individuals and the activities carried on in a community. For this reason, idealist philosophies which tend to construe everything as an aspect of a whole appeal strongly to religious emotions. The natural bent of religious thought is towards a unity in which all things are incorporated and each individual recognizes himself not as the centre of the world (as his egoism sometimes suggests) but as a fragment of some larger scheme of things. The fundamental emotion of religions is some form of piety: that is, a recognition that the world, and especially certain parts of it (temples, sacred animals, perhaps other human beings) is not simply something to be used according to the desires of the moment. To be religious is to be constantly recognizing a movement of thought between the appreciation of this larger scheme of things on the one hand, and the set of distractions (such as lust, ambition, heedless desires, mere forgetfulness) to which all human beings are prone, and which in Christianity is called sin. The essence of sin is that it is fragmentary: it is a response to a part of the universe and not to the whole. In order to maintain an appropriate form of awareness (or 'consciousness') rituals and prayers are instituted: they focus the mind on the required coherence. Without such a focus we live, as the Preacher says in *Ecclesiastes*, amidst vanities.

Religion, then, is so closely associated with morality and with the popular meaning of philosophy as to be for all practical purposes (and religion *is* entirely a matter of practical purposes) indistinguishable from them. A Regulus who, captured by the Carthaginians, advised the Romans to continue to fight the war and was consequently barbarously put to death by them became a heroic legend. It matters not that the story is probably not true, nor whether we regard him as a patriotic hero or a religious one. The historical truth is as unimportant, from a religious point of view, as the distinction between the political and the spiritual: religion, for the Romans as for most other peoples, is not to be identified with the spiritual but is rather what binds the spiritual and the political together. Above all, truth is not particularly important, because religion deals not in truth but in the very different matter of 'saving truths'. It is here, particularly, that Christianity is a misleading guide to these matters.

For it has recently come to be a charge of reproach hurled at religions that they are 'empirically vacuous'. They commonly assert things about invisible powers. These invisible powers are generally personified as God, or gods, but there is no reason why personification should be taken as essential. Metaphysical forces and influences will do as well and are commonly found, as for example in various forms of occultism. Further, religions assert commands and prohibitions; but it would be simply confused to look for empirical content here. Religions prescribe ritual, and they announce what is valuable. In other words, a perfectly adequate religion may be made up of no other set of beliefs than these, and may therefore be, quite legitimately, 'empirically vacuous'. Most religions developed, of course, long before anybody bothered about empirical vacuity, and most included a cognitive thrust which took them far beyond religious concerns into asserting statements in areas of curiosity where the truth was not and could not then be known. Imagination, as it were, required an answer long before reason could supply one. Hence it is that all sophisticated religions acquired a cosmology which, resting upon common sense, asserted that the earth was the centre of the universe and everything revolved around it. Here was a sensible doctrine which any sensible man could verify merely by using his eyes. It happens that the belief is false, and educated men remember well a number of painful episodes in which Christianity disembarrassed itself of this doctrine. Similarly, a literal interpretation of the Old Testament suggested possible views of man's creation and his life on this planet which have been taken as contradictory to Darwinian natural selection, and also to the archaeological dating which suggests that human history goes back rather further than the date of 4004 BC which Archbishop Ussher extracted from the Bible. But this kind of conflict between religion and science – the kind of conflict which is necessary if a religion is *not* to be empirically vacuous – has nothing at all to do with religion. The notion that the writers of the book of Genesis were presenting a hypothesis in the field of prehistory, or one about animal species, is entirely ludicrous, and there can be very few people who now hold it.

Similarly, it is a mistake to identify religion with a belief in God or gods. For one thing, many religions put much less stress upon what is believed than others; for another, the idea of God is a very common solution to a religious problem but it is not an inevitable one. There are many religious people who would no doubt argue that any form of religious thinking that does not arrive at the idea of a God who created the world has not faced up to what is involved in the human situation. A belief in divinity may certainly be advanced as one of the criteria for a satisfactory religion, but it cannot be allowed to determine the entire category. Error often arises on this point because Europeans tend to assimilate religion to science: a rationalist civilization assumes everything to begin with knowledge or belief, from which practice is thought to follow. This assumption must be reversed if we are to understand religion. The demand that religions should not be empirically vacous and the identification of religion with belief in God both result from the assumption that religion must essentially be a kind of knowledge: but to make religion a kind of science is certain to make it a science *manqué*.

It should perhaps be added that although this argument does not present the view of religion commonly occurring in controversial discussion it is an eminently common and traditional view of the matter : 'Devotion to some principle; strict fidelity or faithfulness; conscientiousness; pious affection or attachment', as the *Shorter Oxford Dictionary* has it. A man's worship, it is commonly said, is where his heart lies, and businessmen have often been accused of the worship of Mammon. And it was common in the nineteenth century to believe that the result of moral regeneration would be that 'religion will once more be understood as the general name for all the worships or habitual admirations which compose the higher life'.[3] Adherence to a religion may indeed be signified by the affirmation of a belief; but it may equally be affirmed by submission to a law or participation in a ritual. Nor are these things integrally connected. Those who participate in the outward actions of a ritual may often have greatly varying beliefs about what it signifies, and obedience to a law does not entail any substantial belief. We may conclude, then, that it is an error to telescope the entire question of religion into the question: Do you believe in God?

It follows from the view I am taking that it is difficult, though not impossible, to be without a religion. Most human beings are strongly inclined to step back on occasion from the daily business of getting and spending in order to consider the wider significance of their lives. Those who do so come up with a variety of answers, some devoting their lives to political causes, others helping the poor, serving humanity by charity, seeking *karma*, attempting to purify their souls or adhering to one of the organized religions or the many cults that exist in society. A great variety of popular beliefs about religion lead a kind of underground life. These things must all be classed as forms of religion. The widespread indifference to Christian belief in Western countries is therefore a misleading guide to the strength of religion, and indeed (though less obviously) also to the strength of Christianity. One of the strongest tenets of Christianity, for example, is that a man's life belongs not to himself but to God, and

[3] J. R. Seeley, *Macmillan's Magazine*, 1879. Quoted in Sheldon Rothblatt, *The Revolution of the Dons*, London 1968.

consequently suicide is taken as a sin and legally discouraged. It was not so in the ancient world, and one might expect that liberal moral beliefs would have led, where men were indifferent to Christianity, to the supersession of this attitude. It is indeed true that attempted suicide is no longer actually punished, nor rewarded with opprobrium; nevertheless a great deal of energy goes into trying to prevent it. Continuity of practice is less evident where justifications vary. One may indeed discern the outlines of new and inarticulate religions in modern life: the view, for example, that each person ought to have a certain number of desirable experiences in his lifetime. Such views may be recognized as merely proto-religious; they remind us that it is possible to pass one's life on a biological escalator, moved by impulse, career, family, appetite and the incessant availability of entertaining distractions, without thought of the wider significance of life. But even this simple kind of life is pressed upon by religion and ritual.

Religion is, then, whatever imaginative apprehension we have of the value of our lives, and while we have seen that it is an error actually to identify religion with belief, it is nevertheless true that religions naturally tend towards the raising of wider questions – tend, that is, towards the pursuit of truth and the development of philosophical issues. In all the more highly evolved world religions we find elements of philosophical speculation alongside a certain awareness of logic. We must not exaggerate, however. Most religions have shown no sign whatever of developing anything like an academic tradition, because their energies have been most directly concentrated not upon truth but upon its practical cousin, wisdom. The question religions always pose is: how ought one to live? And the answer is always in terms of a way or path which is intellectually supported by speculative principles (ideas of Nature, of higher and lower powers, of different fundamental principles of the universe) which have always been framed for their relevance to the spiritual path. Very frequently, this intellectual elaboration has been arrived at by leaps of insight, mystical intuitions or illuminating paradoxes. Intellectually speaking, then, religion may pose intellectual questions, and therefore may tempt some religious thinkers away from wisdom towards a disinterested concern for truth, quite irrespective of how men ought to live. And although such a derailment of religious attention rarely happens, it is difficult to see any other way in which academic inquiry could happen at all. For religion is that part of practical life where the widest horizons are likely to appear.

From an academic point of view the religious concern for wisdom is an intellectual failure, while from a religious point of view academic inquiry – logic, mathematics, cosmology, pursued in a disinterested spirit – is merely a diversion from a man's main problem, which is how to live.[4] There comes a point when the academic and religious roads must diverge: academic inquiry will begin to press on and to destroy what religion finds it salutary to take for granted. This difference leads on to further divergences: the apex of religious activity is the wise man or guru, whose business it is in part to baffle and perplex his disciples in a way which would be found intolerable within the academic tradition. In religious terms 'understanding' is an experience of which the possessor may not be able to give any very lucid account, while within the academic tradition nothing can be counted as understanding which cannot be explained. Understanding is defined in terms of public availability. Differences in the ability to understand are merely contingent in the academic world; they are essential in the religious sphere. From all of this, it follows that the typical form of religious teaching is a guru with his disciples, men whose faith in the superiority of the master is absolute and who will be dedicated to find-

[4] What Gibbon attributes to the early Fathers of the Church is true of the religious attitude in general: 'The acquisition of knowledge . . . may employ the leisure of a liberal mind. Such amusements, however, were rejected with abhorrence or admitted with the utmost caution by the severity of the fathers, who despised all knowledge that was not useful to salvation. . . .' *Decline and Fall of the Roman Empire*, ch. XV.

ing wisdom in whatever he says. It will be axiomatic that if what the master says appears base, or foolish, or nonsensical, then it has not been fully understood. Someone engaged in academic inquiry could not but regard such an attitude as an irritating form of servility. Each wise man is complete in himself, while an academic inquirer must see himself as essentially part of a cooperative enterprise in which the limitations of each person's understanding are supplemented by the aid of others. Universities must treat as open and disputable matters which seem (at least superficially) to be the same as those which religion treats as settled. Truths tend to be competitive, for on any properly formulated issue there can only be one; but 'saving truths' can be multiple and live in perfect harmony with each other. It was primarily a philosophical not a religious impulse which led Abelard and his contemporaries to be concerned at the intellectual incoherence of inherited Christian beliefs.

These matters will appear in a clearer focus if we consider what it is that makes Christianity a rather odd kind of religion. For although the academic tradition may be seen emerging at other times than the medieval (in classical Greece, for example) there can be little doubt that with us it owes much of its strength to certain peculiarities of Christianity. For Christianity is a peculiarly intellectual religion. Part of the reason is, no doubt, that it fell into the hands of Greeks and Jews of an especially disputatious temperament. A further influence may well be an association between the jealousy of the old Testament God and the exclusiveness of the single possible truth. But the main cause of intellectuality was the fact that Christianity was the religion of a self-selecting group of outsiders in the Roman Empire. It was not the religion of a natural community, but of an artificial community constituted by an act of belief. Further, being but one religion among many of a similar type, it developed a strong sense of the intellectual *minutiae* by which a Christian was to be distinguished from a syncretizing heathen. The price of indifference to heresy was

extinction. The measure of their cohesiveness was the extent
to which they embraced their role as *peregrini*: resident
aliens whose belief made them citizens of another world
altogether. But they were very determined to build themselves a church on earth. The political triumph of this
attitude may be dated from AD 379, when the Emperor
Theodosius imposed uniformity of belief upon Christians by
imperial decree. Gibbon comments that:

> The secretaries were gradually disqualified for the possession
> of honorable or lucrative employments; and Theodosius was satis-
> fied with his own justice when he decreed that as the Eunomians
> distinguished the nature of the Son from that of the Father, they
> should be incapable of making their wills, or of receiving any
> advantage from testamentary donations. The guilt of the
> Manichaean heresy was esteemed of such magnitude that it could
> be expiated only by the death of the offender; and the same
> capital puishment was inflicted on the Audians, or *Quartodoci-
> mans*, who should dare to perpetrate the atrocious crime of
> celebrating on an improper day the festival of Easter.[5]

A second significant feature of Christianity is its
individuality, something closely related to the early political
circumstances which we have just discussed. It is explicitly
concerned not with the prospects of any actual political
community but with the worth and destiny of the individual
soul. How and why this emphasis emerged is a complicated
and fascinating question,[6] but it certainly set considerable
problems for later Christian thinkers, and must be accounted
the most important element of the situation which led from
early medieval times onward to a continuing flowering of
individuality which has created the modernity of the current
world and in particular the idea that rights attach to the
individual personality. Among the many impulses fused to-

---

[5] *The Decline and Fall of the Roman Empire*, ch. XXVII. The passage is quoted in
Elie Kedourie, *Nationalism in Asia and Africa*, New York 1970, p. 31, where the
political significance of the demand for uniformity of belief is also considered.
[6] A brilliant discussion of it may be found in Charles Norris Cochrane, *Christianity
and Classical Culture*, Oxford 1940.

gether in this complex idea is the belief that each individual's beliefs have a certain claim to attention on the minimal ground that he holds them. For whereas most people in the world are born into their religions, the Christian is required at least in principle to make various optional affirmations of faith. This individuality does not contradict the position that each person remains fragmentary, which Christianity shares with other religions: each person is related to the larger scheme of things not by membership of a political community but by membership of a church.

The idea of a church is a third significant distinction of Christianity: the spiritual and political realms are separate and are governed by separate authorities. This makes Christianity an other-worldly religion in a way that most other religions are not, and it opens up a gulf between heaven and earth which has caused an almost incessant rumbling of discontent among both believers and critics. One consequence of the gulf is that European history is a story of struggles between two more or less co-ordinate authorities; and this conflict has allowed very great freedom to other social institutions, including universities. Had feudal Europe not consisted of a large number of authorities in frequent conflict with each other, the history of the freedom of thought would have been very different.

The churches of Christendom have had to deal with enemies in almost every generation of their existence. Apart from heresy and paganism, there has been a strong strain of anticlericalism. Indeed, our whole understanding of these important matters has been entirely distorted because, in the last two centuries, powerful attacks on Christianity have been made by men who cherished the illusion that they were the voice of reason attacking religion and superstition. It is never wise to take people at their own valuation, and in this case it leads to a palpable error. For what is it that can attack a religion like Christianity? If the attack is on Christian social policies, then it is not an attack upon religion but upon the political tendencies of the Church, and these have been somewhat variable: no politics is directly implied by a religion whose kingdom is not of this world. And if the attack comes in the name of truth, what are we to make of it? For reasons which will become clearer in the chapter after next, it is in the strict sense impossible for a religious affirmation to contradict a scientific hypothesis: they are in different moods and have different significations. It is true, of course, that if a Church chooses to assert as a dogma propositions which seem to run counter to the strongly argued conclusions of scientific inquiry then a real conflict can arise: and at various times this has happened. But such a conflict rests, essentially, upon a misunderstanding of religion. It is also true that to the extent to which a religion rests its fortune upon a theology, then it may suffer from the attention of philosophers, who may diagnose internal contradiction. It may have to suffer its 'proofs' of the existence of God reduced to nullity, and the problem of evil will obviously pose difficulties for those who believe in both the omnipotence and the benevolence of God. Nonetheless, in so far as these matters are discussed academically they can never issue in a decisive conclusion. It would be an absurdity to imagine that philosophical theology will ever culminate in a moment when everyone rises up from the seminar, saying either that 'God's existence has been proved' or that 'God's existence has been disproved'. Ordinary believers are, in any case, not philosophers; they may well be happy to believe *because* the thing is absurd, and they are not taking up a demonstrably irrational position if they retreat to the view that God's purposes are altogether too mysterious for human minds to fathom.

It would seem then that any kind of academic criticism of Christianity (as of any religion at all) can do no better than nibble at it around the edges. In spite of this, men using apparently academic devices have mounted a large and powerful attack on Christianity and sought to exhibit it as a demeaning piece of superstitious wish-fulfilment inherited from darker days. This movement ranges from the Hegelian sophistication of a Feuerbach to ranting on the soapbox. In

43

other words, anti-Christian argument has met Christian apologetics at every level of sophistication. This attack has been conducted in the name of Reason and Progress, but in terms of our argument it will be clear that this movement can be regarded as constituted of nothing else but one or more alternative religions. For any powerful argument which is relevantly directed against a religious belief must itself be a form of religious belief, and only the curious circumstances of Western intellectuality have prevented this fact from being entirely evident. We associate religion with belief in God, and whoever simply opposes such a belief with what he claims to be rational arguments looks superficially like an inquirer rather than the apostle of an alternative religion. Again, science has lent its authority to an intellectual programme of discouraging belief in invisible entities. It has thus been the sad fate of many previously respectable species of spirit – leprechauns, fairies, hobgoblins, etc – to be demoted from the temple to the nursery. Most modern Europeans have believed that all respectable beliefs ought to look like science or philosophy, and critics of Christianity could present themselves under the shelter of that respectable rubric. The result has been that the religious impulses of modern Europeans have suffered the fate of an unconfident child whose performances are watched by a domineering father. Robespierre could convert churches into temples for the worship of the Supreme Being, but the cult of a Lenin or a Mao must look like spontaneous and rational respect for intelligence and achievement.

In the struggle against Christianity, what has been the fate of the three characteristics which, we have suggested, distinguish Christianity from most other religions? The first of these, intellectuality, has been taken over by virtually all candidates for the religious succession. All of them believe, as do Christians, that they are the possessors of an exclusive and impeccable revelation, and most of them have become efficient at sniffing out heresy. A totalitarian state is a kind of grotesque caricature of a Christian Com-

monwealth, in that its unity rests not only upon an imposed
uniformity of belief but also upon a demanded uniformity
of enthusiasm.

The other two characteristics have, however, fared very
differently. Indeed, their fate has to some extent gone together. It was St Augustine who, early in the Christian era,
had to argue against educated Romans' nostalgia for the
unified and martial gods of the Roman past, and in this controversy, as in most, neither side has ever managed to secure
a decisive victory. For many centuries Augustine's theological successors were paralleled by classical republicans
who looked back to a time when civil society had its own
civil religion and authority was not split between the
spiritual and the temporal realms. Machiavelli, a prominent
writer of this tradition, supplies us with one version of the
attack on Christianity in which both its individuality and its
split with the political realm are simultaneously deplored. 'I
love my native city more than my own soul', he wrote in a
famous letter composed late in life; and he praised
Florentines who, from their anti-Papal behaviour, seemed to
have acted on the same sentiment. Machiavelli was certainly no enemy of individualism, but he largely took it to
be the pursuit of fame. He regarded humility and a life
devoted to personal salvation as a sentiment appropriate to
slaves. Many later writers have done the same. But this is a
difficult and treacherous subject, for slavishness may be diagnosed either in individuality or in hatred of it, according to
the meaning given to this slippery term. It has certainly been
the case that one strong anti-Christian trend has associated
individuality and Christianity with a capitalist society domin-
ated by money values and, in particular, the bourgeois class.
Individuality has been taken as the characteristic which sets
man against man in, if not deadly enmity, at least cut-throat
competition, and reformers have sought to supplant it with
a fraternal and comradely relation between man and man.
And in all cases where this change has been attempted, the

45

state has become the centre of a cult and has been greatly strengthened.

Our understanding of these matters has been obscured by the fact that Christianity, itself a strange religion, has generated heresies equally strange. The heretic and the heathen may be found in many religious circumstances, and it has commonly happened that philosophy, taken as an esoteric inquiry conducted more or less privately, has come into conflict with religion. This happened in Greece (where part of the offence was, of course, that of bringing philosophy into the market place); and it also happened among the Arab scholars during the early centuries of Islamic intellectual vigour.[7] Attacks upon particular religious doctrines have, therefore, been very common indeed, but an attack upon 'religion' in general is a novel and, in one sense, impossible project. Both parties to the dispute must therefore be counted as imposters. Christianity is no more to be identified with 'religion' than agnosticism, humanism, atheism or communism are to be counted as Reason, Science or Philosophy. And these intellectual conflicts, far from testifying to the weakness of religion in the modern world, testify rather to its strength.

This kind of argument is sometimes advanced in a debunking spirit, but it should be clear that no element of attack can be involved in my argument. For on the view I am taking it is very difficult for men to be without a religion, though they may have to make do with a somewhat incoherent jumble of beliefs culled from disparate sources. It is also true that the conclusions of the intellectual conflict known as Religion versus Science have been such as to influence men not towards mankind's vast stock of existing religious ideas but rather towards the conversion into a saving truth of some other set of beliefs currently found circulating in the intellectual world. Religions have to take on the look of sciences, and some actually resort to such desperate and foolish stratagems as to claim that in one or

[7] See Leo Strauss, *Persecution and the Art of Writing*, Glencoe 1952.

other of their doctrines they have anticipated this or that current scientific hypothesis. When some fragments of the academic world have been split off in this way to form theologies, the result is that commonest of modern intellectual constructions, an ideology. A scientific façade to a religion is, of course, merely a persuasive device, and makes a religion neither better nor worse – except that if the façade be taken for the building it will cause extensive distortion in our understanding of the structure of knowledge.

We may now sum this argument up: the academic tradition is tangentially related to certain of the religious preoccupations of mankind. Literature, history and philosophy all arose in this way, but philosophy has been central. 'In the history of human inquiry', as J. L. Austin has remarked, 'philosophy has the place of the initial central sun, seminal and tumultuous: from time to time it throws off some portion of itself to take station as a science, a planet, cool and well regulated, progressing steadily towards a distant final state.'[8] Although this may be described as an illuminating account of a very complicated process, we should do well to abandon seminal suns in favour of the more humdrum analogy of the family, for while planets do not quarrel with the sun, children do quarrel with the parents, and in the incompatibility between the religious and the academic attitudes we have the cause of the abundant conflicts to which our annals testify. Logically speaking, this conflict is generally the result of a confusion, for the bearing of a religious dogma upon an academic suggestion is so slight that the two things hardly meet. But it has certainly been true that men in successive generations have believed that such a conflict is real, and in order to moderate it, universities have brought forth demands for academic freedom.

The academic tradition is in this respect, as in many, the inheritor of the classical situation of philosophy. For

<hr/>

[8] 'Ifs and Cans', *ad fin.* Reprinted in J. N. Findlay (ed.), *Studies in Philosophy: British Academy Lectures*, London 1966, p. 141.

wherever philosophy has developed beyond the custodian-
ship of priests, it has always produced understandings of
the world which might be taken as subversive. This is true
equally of the Christian, Judaic and Islamic religions. The
discovery of such a truth, for example, as that moral standards and attitudes are widely variable according to time
and place carries no implication for behaviour whatever. But
it can certainly be used in a rhetorical argument justifying
defiance of some current standard as being merely customary. As a piece of justification, such a proposition is no longer
academic or philosophical, and it therefore comes within the
area of what almost all governments have felt themselves
warranted in regulating. Governments, like all responsible
bodies, are of a nervous disposition, and prefer not to take
risks with stability. For reasons we shall later discuss, it is
often painful to men's peace of mind to have to tolerate the
expression of opinions they regard as subversive. This is clear
enough even in a liberal society, where impious beliefs have
lost their power to shock because they are so abundant. But
it is even more intensely true where the moral health of the
community is thought to rest upon everyone sharing certain
required pieties. Such a situation is obviously likely to
restrict academic inquiry: both because academics may be
sceptical of the required belief, and on the more general
ground that universities tend towards scepticism in all fields.
In considering academic freedom, we may distinguish three
types of relationship between a government and its
universities.

The first and much the commonest position is where the
orthodoxy is enforced throughout society without recognition of academic boundaries. This is the case in totalitarian
states; it has generally been the case in all the despotisms of
the east, and it has often prevailed wherever the Christian
Church has become a department of state exercising tutorial
responsibilities to its populations. In these circumstances,
anything recognizable as academic freedom is the result of
the inadvertence of the powerful or the prudence of the

philospher. Even the most desperate despot sometimes sleeps.

The second possibility is the recognition of the academic sphere as something which ought to be left alone so long as it remains politically neutral. The story was told in the eighteenth century how Louis xiv's minister Colbert called together some of the merchants of Paris and, in mercantilist style, asked them how the government could best aid them in bringing about the commercial prosperity of France. Eventually one merchant growled: 'Laissez-nous faire.' Governments bent on regulation have often recognized trade as an area which is best left to thrive unregulated. A similar attitude may prevail in respect to universities, and it may be necessary even in the freest of countries. Any sensible government will recognize that a professor of anatomy discoursing upon the structure of the sexual organs ought not to suffer whatever penalties have been decreed for the pornographer. And this kind of situation – where it is clearly recognized that academic inquiry requires certain specific immunities from the ordinary law – is the paradigm of academic freedom. Where there are many cases of this kind, the distinction between the academic and the practical worlds is clearly recognized.

These two situations are much the commonest in human experience, but it happens that we are most familiar with a third. A liberal society (which commonly tends also to have a democratic constitution) is one which has achieved something long unusual in European experience: it has relegated all forms of religious belief to the realm of private judgement. A liberal state is not thought to rest upon any serious homogeneity of belief, but upon the quite different basis of a formal allegiance to precise constitutional modes of political change. Power comes (not out of the barrel of a gun but) out of a complicated set of constitutional practices which are regarded as superior to any particular belief which anyone might hold. This description of a liberal society also indicates the condition of its continuance, for the moment people hold some belief as being so important that, rather than suffer frustration, they are prepared to resort to bombs, then this kind of society will collapse back into one or other of the first two usages described. Indeed, the triumph of *any* belief thought more important than constitutional procedures of change is incompatible with a liberal situation. Now what distinguishes a liberal situation is that the civil liberty to express any opinion becomes coterminous with the academic requirement that any hypothesis should be capable of being entertained. Academic freedom thus ceases to be wider than freedom of speech, and this latter right is indifferently accorded to everyone, subject only to such laws as those of libel, slander and incitement to breach of the peace. Academic freedom is like a diplomatic immunity: an exemption from the rigour of law, granted as necessary to the performance of an activity. But where such exemptions are universally available, they cease to be significant.

3 Lectures, Dons and Undergraduates: Institutional Resilience

The survival of universities over eight centuries is an astonishing, fragile and (it may be) temporary achievement. For most of the time, they have been cities under siege. Although stoutly built as part of the medieval realm, they have often been damaged because they were seen either as a threat to some preoccupation in society at large or, alternatively, as a resource too valuable to be left alone. Whoever has conceived some powerful enthusiasm has almost immediately set to work constructing appropriate siege machines. Dominant churches have sought to subdue universities to a doctrine, and governments have been eager to control their teaching and membership. The celebrated twentieth-century attacks are crude instances of something which is much more menacing when done by stealth. The Nazi party's enthusiasm for freeing the universities from the shackles of decadent Jewish scholarship is and was easily recognized as unacademic; and the belief current under the rule of Stalin that all wisdom was a deduction from Marxist-Leninist dialectics is no very serious intellectual menace to the vitality of European civilization, however politically unpleasant. The real threat, which has at times overrun various suburbs of Academe, comes from outside enthusiasms dressed up as if they were academic beliefs. It is this kind of besieger, operating often from within the walls, which will be our main concern in later chapters.

The vitality of universities may partly be measured by the extent to which they have survived the nervous feelings they often arouse in practical men. And a large part of that vitality resides – so we shall argue in this chapter – in familiar features of academic organization which have mostly been inherited from the Middle Ages. Political attack and academic defence : such has been exactly the rhythm of the history of universities. For they have never themselves initiated an attack on the outside world. This argument depends upon logical considerations which will emerge only when we consider the academic and the practical worlds. But it seems obvious even on the face of things that the scholarly concerns of universities were always tangential to the social and political conflicts of Europe. This is not to deny, of course, that every don is also a citizen, and that citizenly sympathies of one kind or another might predominate in some colleges. This certainly happened in the English civil war, Puritans regarding the universities as little more than wings of the established church, while Hobbes and many of the royalists regarded them as strongholds of republican and Calvinist enthusiasm. Carried away by such preoccupations, Hobbes, an unfilial child of the classics, spoke for men in many generations when he wrote: 'There was never anything so dearly bought, as these western parts have bought the learning of the Greek and Latin tongues.'[1] Just as many contemporary defenders of the classics unwisely base their case upon classical literature being an inducement to liberal and democratic attitudes, so Hobbes attributed rebellion against the monarchy to the 'reading of books of policy and histories of the ancient Greeks, and Romans'.[2] The irony, of course, is that many of Hobbes's absolutist convictions seem to have derived from his immersion in the account of human affairs rendered by Thucydides. Hobbes believed

[1] *Leviathan*, ch. 21.
[2] Ibid., ch. 29.

that universities should play their proper role in a single political realm of which all components supported the authority of the sovereign. This gave universities an important, if dependent, position in the state, for 'the instruction of the people, dependeth wholly, on the right teaching of youth in the universities.'[3]

From about the same period, universities have been subject to ceaseless grumbling because they have failed to participate in what one set of enthusiasts regarded as mankind's compulsory adventure: exploiting the resources of the earth. Practical men have noticed that the study of Latin and Greek is not always an inducement to a business career, and may even dampen commercial enthusiasm. Nor is this attitude confined to practical men. 'Can there be anything more ridiculous', Locke wrote, 'than that a father should waste his own money, and his son's time, in setting him to *learn the Roman language,* when at the same time he *designs him for a trade,* wherein he, having no use of Latin, fails not to forget that little which he brought from school, and which 'tis ten to one he abhors for the ill-usage it procured him?' This attitude challenges not merely the classics but any kind of academic education at all. Newman's *Idea of a University* argues against this kind of practical attitude which flourished in the nineteenth century under the banner of Utility. 'This process of training', he wrote in *Discourse VII,* 'by which the intellect, instead of being formed or sacrificed to some particular or accidental purpose, some specific trade or profession, or study or science, is disciplined for its own sake, for the perception of its own proper object, and for its own highest culture, is called Liberal Education.' In the century since Newman wrote in this vein, the universities have been pushed steadily in the direction of providing professional and vocational training; or, to continue the metaphor of siege, Society has successfully subdued large areas of the university.

The utilitarian distrust of the academic has in the last

[3] Ibid., ch. 30.

century been crossed with the clamour of the class war, and brought forth a new and active type of critic who seeks to subdue the universities because he can see in them nothing else but citadels of privilege. Max Weber once argued that the function of religion was to be 'a service of legitimation ... for the external and inner interests of all ruling men, the propertied, the victorious and the healthy'.[4] This account of religion is precisely what utilitarian and radical critics take the university to be. Anyone who has assented to the argument of the previous chapter, according to which the religious and the academic are distinct and indeed antipathetic, will find this particular shuffling of categories puzzling. What we confront, however, is a critic for whom the notion of 'class-implication' is a fundamental touchstone of all judgement: a touchstone, in other words, of a political and religious character; and religions, by and large, are blind to anything else except other religions. One recent critic of the universities, basing himself upon what he takes to be the needs and tendencies of modern society, thinks that the conflict of educational ideas 'can be resolved only by breaking the domination of the whole educational system by universities which are devoted to the academic ideal'.[5] This is a declaration of war, partly explained by the dustjacket's assertion that the universities are 'amongst the last strongholds of elitist education'. Another critic writing in the same vein expresses the tone of much of this attack when he writes:

To put it crudely, the British universities are aloof, exclusive, conservative, scholastic and middle class. Their independence is preserved by the University Grants Committee; they are unresponsive to social and industrial demand (it took the Robbins Committee and all those appendices to make them accept the previous expansion); they are concerned with the preservation, extension and dissemination of knowledge for its own sake (even ostensibly vocational sources [sic] like engineering require subsequent prac-

[4] H. H. Gerth and C. Wright Mills (eds), *From Max Weber*, Oxford 1946, p. 240.
[5] Eric Robinson, *The New Polytechnics*, London 1969, p. 92.

tical experience before a man is qualified); their students are almost all studying full-time for a first degree and are of a class composition which has been surprisingly similar for fifty years.[6]

This is part of an argument for the expansion and development of alternative forms of tertiary education, but this attitude is commonly combined with the ambition to transform universities into something else. Such attacks, which have a long history, make it very clear that universities have *not* been 'more or less responsive to national need'.

An institution so continuously invested in this way needs sources of strength in order to resist. In a later section, we shall be concerned with those elements of academic resilience which reside in its outside connection. Here we are concerned with some of the benefits of its institutional inheritance. Some of these elements – that of academic self-government, for example – are obviously of the first importance and have been widely discussed. But there are equally evident features of academic institutions whose importance is less widely recognized.

Consider, as one example, the lecturing system, and take for a typical critic not the kind of modern radical who identifies sitting in silence for an hour with 'passivity' or 'inertness', but rather the urbane and cultivated Aldous Huxley, always a good man to illustrate a rationalist prejudice :

> Lecturing as a method of instruction dates from classical and mediaeval times, before the invention of printing. When books were worth their weight in gold, professors had to lecture. Cheap printing has radically changed the situation which produced the lecturer of antiquity. And yet—preposterous anomaly!—the lecturer survives and even flourishes. In all the universities of Europe his voice still drones and brays just as it droned and brayed in the days of Duns Scotus and Thomas Aquinas. Lecturers are as much an anachronism as bad drains or tallow candles; it is high time they were got rid of.[7]

[6] Tyrrell Burgess, *Sunday Times*, 4 October 1970.
[7] *Proper Studies*, London 1927, p. 133.

Mr Huxley's assumption that everything belonging to the past should be got rid of would indeed leave the universities sinking uder the tides of time. But what *is* an anachronism? As historians usefully employ the term, it is something which *could* not exist at a particular time. When the word is domesticated to moral and political use, and taken to mean something which merely *ought* not to exist, then it sinks to the level of a sentence of exile passed by an irritable judge upon some feature of the world which has displeased him. It becomes an instrument of fantasy. Underlying the fantasy, however, we may discern a type of argument which has often been used as a battering ram in the siege of academe. Rather like a mechanical device, this argument selects some feature of university organization, assigns to it some plausible cause, points then to the fact that the supposed cause no longer operates, and thus reveals the feature as a dangling tribute to mankind's capacity for clinging to old habits. Huxley's argument is a mere *jeu d'esprit,* an entertaining exaggeration which he hardly takes seriously, for his intention is to shock and amuse. There are plenty of other critics who are very serious indeed about understanding such things as lectures as being essentially no more than what they appear : a way of telling people things. It is certainly true that as a device for transmitting information lectures are absurdly inefficient. Any student can read a published lecture in a fraction of the time it takes to deliver it. But this does not take us very far.

The clue to the real character of lectures may be found in Plato's argument, in the *Seventh Letter,* that there are some things which cannot suitably be written down, and that the tradition of inquiry must pass from pupil to master like a spark. He no doubt meant a great deal by this image; but part of what he meant is that a tradition of learning is not simply a quantum of information, but a certain attitude to it — a set of *nuances* which appear in the tone of voice that is used and in the choice of things to be qualified along the path of the exposition. A lecture, to adapt an old legal maxim, is a speaking book, and those who listen to a lecture are absorbing, partly consciously and partly unconsciously, a certain manner of reading books and treating the information they acquire.

Seen in this light, a lecture is a ceremonial device for diffusing some particular tradition of learning: it deals with a subject conceived not abstractly as the set of assertions that might usefully be found in a textbook or an encyclopedia, but as the intellectual resources by which a continuing inquiry into some aspect of things is being conducted. It is true that wherever classes and tutorials abound – as is often the case in British universities – lectures are a less necessary way of rendering a subject 'vivid' in this sense. But something of this sort must exist, for it is by his grip upon the vividness of a subject that an educated man is to be distinguished from the self-taught man who has applied himself to books. Although differing native abilities produce wide variations, the man whose learning has come exclusively from books is at the mercy of whatever level of knowledge there is when he acquires his learning. The *raison d'être* of universities is, by contrast, to pass on the kind of tentative and exploratory understanding which leads academics to regard most books as merely progress reports.

On this ground, lectures, tutorials and classes might all take their place more or less indifferently as ways of bringing students into contact with the living current of a subject. In other respects, however, the lecture has a certain pre-eminence. For the duty of giving lectures is a pressure upon the academic to rethink what he takes to be the fundamentals of his subject every year that he has to give them. This fact is a clue to the nature of universities, a clue which is worth following because many people have been seduced by such metaphors as that of 'the frontiers of knowledge' into believing that universities are pre-eminently places where 'advanced' studies are pursued. This manner of thinking suggests that way back in the 'centre' of knowledge there is something secure and fixed. This is a superficial and popular view. The real distinction of universities is that they are unusual combinations of 'advanced' work, on the one hand, with the continuous rethinking and restatement of many things which, for all practical purposes, we take for granted. They deal as much with simplicities as complexities. The ordinary lectures for the undergraduates are, then, not merely exhibitions revealing to students how someone who is presumed to know a great deal about a subject goes about giving an account of some part of it; they are also rituals which force scholars to re-examine their subject as a whole, and therefore a significant complement to minute or specialized researches. For in academic terms, to teach a subject is to rethink it; and the problems of rethinking it often become far more evident in the preparation of lectures than in tutorial or classroom discussion.

These considerations need not prevent us from recognizing that there is some truth in the complaint which led Aldous Huxley to his belief that lecturing was an 'anachronism': 'At most universities', he wrote in 1927, and the situation has hardly changed since, 'an entirely disproportionate importance is attached to lectures. Students are compelled to attend innumerable courses, and it is made difficult, often impossible, for a man – however intelligent or well informed – to obtain a degree who has not attended these courses, and is therefore unable to reproduce, parrot-fashion, the favourite ideas and phrases of the lecturing professor.' It is certainly true that what may be said in defence of the institution of the lecture – and of some lectures – by no means covers all the lecturing arrangements that may exist at different times and places. There are plenty of bad, dull, incompetent lecturers who bring to their entirely familiar material little but the monotony of their voices and the peripheral quibbling by which alone they demonstrate their academic quality. But here we run into familiar problems of judging any human performance: there is by no means always agreement that such and such a set of lectures is dull and unprofitable. Universities have generally taken the view that it is better to allow such lectures to continue than to entrust to anyone the dangerous task of weeding out the incompetent lecturers – largely because it is often difficult to judge these matters conclusively, and there are very few sets of lectures which find no audience at all.

Indeed, the situation is much more difficult than this sketch has indicated. For while it is often easy to judge – or at least people *do* easily judge – that some lectures are stimulating and others a waste of time, there are many sets of lectures which have a deceptive appearance of excellence, and which are popular with students, but which are of little academic significance. Lectures in universities are sometimes judged as performances in public speaking; and what is admirable in these terms – being coherent, well-organized, interspersed with appropriately humorous remarks and full of useful information – can nonetheless be misleading to students as failing to communicate to the intelligent undergraduate any sense of evolving thought. The main virtue of a lecture is to reveal something of what goes on behind the scenes of academic inquiry – even if it be only a sense of the hesitations and discarded alternatives which can seldom appear on the surface of books. On this assumption, the commonly held view that university teachers ought to be taught techniques of public speaking is in danger of destroying precisely what may be uniquely valuable in academic lectures. No doubt there are some lectures, and some teaching in universities, where the sole point *is* simply to communicate facts and techniques; and where this is true there can be no objection to improvements which permit this to be done more efficiently. These improvements are no less useful for being marginal : speaking up, facing the audience, speaking faster or slower: But in the lecturing which is most specifically academic, the only kind of technique that may be taught by educationalists must necessarily also be the sort of gloss which obscures what is personal and specific to the subject in question.

This view of lecturers suggests an important criterion for an academic subject : that it must be sufficiently complex to bear the weight of such subtleties. Philosophy has always been recognized as a paradigm of academic inquiry, while such skills as driving or domestic science are essentially practical skills. They must be cultivated in a practical manner, for no academic training directly engenders practical skills. But between these extremes there are many difficult judgements to be made, and in the last century a great liberalization of attitude has come about. Science, history and the vernacular literatures, not to mention industrial and agricultural technologies, have all been widely admitted, and in various places the university has come close to becoming (what many regard as an ideal) a kind of community centre where all skills may be learned and all things talked about.

Universities can only preserve their identity if they steer by the compass of the academic; without it, their increasing involvement with society makes them the helpless pursuers of incoherent desirabilities. The choice they face is between losing themselves in an intellectual chaos, where fashion and social need are powerful unacademic forces, or clinging fast to what is reliably traditional and thus dying from ossification. The admission of new subjects raises peculiarly difficult problems of university government.

In many corners of the academic world, embryonic forms of inquiry encourage high hopes, even though their present results are rudimentary and banal if compared with established disciplines. Outside pressures and pervasive fashions dictate the adoption of trivial subjects (which may well deal with questions of great practical urgency) presented as promising by a suitable salvo of academic programmatics. The expulsion of alchemy and astrology, the admission of social science or creative writing raise questions of this kind. Many branches of the social sciences have been living off the presumed splendour of their futures for as long as anyone can remember. Academic programmatics of this kind set up a Baconian scheme of data-collection ('we know surprisingly little about ... hardly any research has been done on . . .') and paint a rosy picture of the higher-order laws which will undoubtedly emerge once the conceptual framework has been agreed and a suitable technical vocabulary, freed from the connotative anarchy of popular discourse, disseminated. But it is logically impossible to know whether such bright ideas will eventually take off into a fully academic sophistication. Again, it has very commonly happened that universities have found themselves the slightly embarrassed recipients of generous endowments for projects associated with some eccentric outside cause. Many chairs in exotic languages have been endowed with the aim of training missionaries for the conversion of the infidel. One of the most successful of the social sciences – anthropology – largely owed its beginning to such non-academic concerns. The lesson to be learned from such incidents is that the organization and ethos of the universities has enormous power, and it has often bent such endowments to the fulfilling of entirely academic purposes. But this lesson is not to be relied on; the combination of huge sums of money with technological enthusiasm will not always be so easily diverted into academic channels.

There is, it is clear, no foolproof way of dealing with these questions. The most careful academic consideration can be misleading. What saves the university from the more extreme consequences of error is its sheer plurality. The universities do not, in most respects, constitute a single system; there are many of them, in many countries, and they contain many individual teachers. Plurality and independence are of their essence, and undoubtedly constitute a reason for their vitality.

It is not that alternative possibilities are lacking. One wise man, surrounded by a band of disciples, is a form of education not unknown in many parts of the world. Men of special learning, or sanctity, or both, have often been able to attract disciples who will sit at their feet. In Europe Plato had his Academy and Aristotle had his Lyceum Indeed this possibly most natural of all kinds of educational transmission was well known in Europe at the time when universities were evolving. In 1263 the *Siete Partidas* issued by King Alfonso the Wise of Castile referred to a master teaching his own pupils as a *studium particulare*, marking it off from a *studium generale*, taken in this context as an association of masters teaching several fields. That the university evolved through the *studium generale* is one of many indications of how deeply the idea of plurality, indeed of free competition, lies at the root of university development. It has always been thought important to prevent the entrenchment of one master, or one academic doctrine, as dominant in the university. Thus medieval manuals refer with disapproval to tendencies among universities to accept as members only those supporting either the realist or the nominalist opinion in metaphysics. A quiet life was not thought worth the intellectual stagnation. For it was clear to medieval scholars, as it is clear to us, that a system of master and disciples will carry with it the strong risk that the master will transmit not only his learning but a good deal of personal idiosyncrasy as well. And the tradition of inquiry has always been seen as something that needs to be kept free of the inevitably personal bias of particular scholars.

Such a bias resembles a deformity of growth. All social institutions suggest analogy with organisms: they are born, they grow, they wax and wane, and all of them seem destined to extinction. This means that they may be judged in terms of their vitality and decadence. It is easy to forget, in making such judgements, that we are dealing with analogies. In an organism, vitality may be identified with some simple physical variable, such as movement or expenditure of energy. To transfer such judgements to human institutions is often misleading, but it has often happened. Decadence and resistence to change have often been attributed to them.

It is significant that universities became decadent virtually as soon as they came into existence. Within the space of the formative twelfth century, the exploratory ferment in Europe's classical inheritance had given way to a series of textbooks – pre-eminently those of Gratian, Irnerius and Peter the Lombard – in which the ordered sequence of question and answer reported the conclusions to subsequent generations. And this codification was followed by a pre-occupation with minutiae and with pedagogic simplification. Here was the first occasion of that hardening of the categories which constantly threatens intellectual endeavour. It was short-lived, for early in the thirteenth century whole new areas of classical work came into Europe from Islam and the Byzantine realm. Within the universities the academic tradition remained lively for a long time after those fruitful additions; indeed, some of the usages of Scholasticism – the dialectical manner and the practice of disputation – were in part designed to maintain vitality and avoid the human temptation of falling into repetition. By the sixteenth and seventeenth centuries – the moment when the rich and aristocratic began to invade the universities in force – Scholasticism was much complained of and seems in some cases to have been but a shadow of its former self. Most of the really distinguished men of the seventeenth century seem to have subscribed to this view of universities. Yet we would do well to be cautious in accepting their complaints. For these men had themselves clearly acquired an education; and most of them were in the grip of an enthusiastic belief that if the business of understanding were undertaken anew, from the very foundations upwards, then momentous achievements were possible. Men in this mood, if they are talented enough, can indeed achieve great things, but they are ill-equipped to recognize their intellectual debts.

Similar judgements about universities have been made recurrently in modern times. In both the eighteenth and the nineteenth centuries Oxford and Cambridge were regarded by many as placid backwaters. Oxford reformed itself after the Act of 1854, and in both universities the unacademic system of leaving most of the teaching to professional coaches fell into disuse. In spite of these reforms, many new

63

institutions of tertiary education were founded in the nineteenth century, particularly technical institutions, and they were often presented as if their main function were to supply the deficiencies of established universities. The true situation is that they were quite properly established in response to demands which it would have been no business of universities to supply.

The charge of decadence brought against universities is, in many cases, nothing more than the propaganda of a cause. Merely to be 'unresponsive to social and industrial demand' often provokes a charge of decadence, immobility, or obsolescence. Similarly, the continued academic investment in old-fashioned subjects like theology and classics has been regarded as an unhealthy addiction to the past by practical men who think that the modern world needs to know more about the chemistry of dyestuffs and the social composition of elites. Even within the university itself, a somewhat vulgar misunderstanding is liable to identify as decadence those periods of academic history which were lacking in celebrated figures writing well-remembered books. Any conception of the university in terms of productivity and output is mistaken, since it assimilates academic inquiry – a thoroughly human activity – to an industrial process in which a regular input of materials which are efficiently combined yields a reliable and homogeneous product. All human activities require times of thought and relaxation, just as human beings require sleep, if they are to sustain their vitality.

Such considerations as these are sufficient to warn us against taking attacks on universities entirely at their face value; one must avoid falling into a response of self-abasement. To fall on one's knees muttering *mea culpa* is one of the great human options open to those who have been accused. It has a perilous attraction for intellectual men rendered over-subtle by their studies. The perfectly real decadence which at times afflicts universities has to be carefully distinguished from the complaints hurled by outside interests whose demands have been ignored.

There is, however, one feature of the academic world which might plausibly be regarded as either vital or decadent according to the consequences considered. This feature is academic tribalism, which occurs whenever some strong-minded intellectual personality sets himself up in a university as a master and gathers around him men who have not the academic character of being fellow-scholars, but the religious character of being disciples. And this fragment of religious terminology so commonly used to describe academic tribalism does indicate a genuine religious element in it. For while academic theories are, strictly speaking, relevant to nothing but other academic theories, it has been possible to adapt to messianic purposes theories first made current in academic theology, philosophy, psychology, history, science or literary criticism. The adoption of a style of thought or a special vocabulary is the common distinguishing mark of an academic tribe. Such tribes often treat their opponents with unfraternal scorn, and watch nervously for heresy within their own ranks. It is not unknown for imitations of the master to extend to physical characteristics – the growing of a moustache or the adoption of a stammer. This is, no doubt, merely the appearance in academic life of that craving for belonging, involving submission to superior power, which is found everywhere in social and political life. It is notable in universities because the activity of intellectual inquiry would seem a barren soil for it. Academic life is always, and rightly, conceived of as a discussion in which there cannot in any circumstances be a final voice; and while churches may need articles of faith and governments will try to propagate a suitable set of agreed legends, it has always been thought a defect in a university to establish and favour one academic doctrine rather than another.

The unsuitability of tribalism to academic life has often been concealed by the unimpeachable respectability of the tribal shibboleths. A tribal leader, on his way to ascendancy, will have rejected the tenets of his elders, and he will commonly justify this in terms of moral beliefs about originality, freedom, criticism, and the virtues of rebellion. These slogans are invariably taken up by the epigoni who repeat, though less profitably, the masters' own rejections. When the fierier statements of the master are repeated with even more passion by the followers, the typical situation has been reached: a posture of rebellion against orthodoxy has become an unrecognized orthodoxy of its own. Such orthodoxies do not belong in a university because they impose an irrelevant outside test to the ideas which may be admitted to intellectual consideration. Here again we have a long-standing feature of academic life which is far from unknown in the outside world. The idea of a 'conformist', for example, used as a term of derogation, could only have been taken up by a set of people who self-consciously prided themselves upon their own individuality, but were content with a mechanical derivation of their unorthodoxy from rejection of what others were doing. Similarly, the injunction: 'think for yourself and don't take things on authority' has been uttered by generations of radical school teachers who have failed to recognize it for the admirably traditional and orthodox precept it really is. In politics, of course, doctrines with their own orthodoxy have managed to persuade their followers that the utterance of aggressive clichés is really a courageous intellectual independence, just as Hitler turned many Germans of his generation into the most docile of sheep by the simple device of explaining to them that biology had made them all lions. These romantic distortions of reality, in which the posture belies the practice, are found as much in the university as they are in the outside world.

Whether academic tribalism is actually decadent is a difficult question we need not tarry to decide. It certainly has many of the stigmata of vitality: enthusiasm and the constant production of writing and speech. Further, it may plausibly be argued that there are many interesting theories whose possibilities could only be explored so long as men were not discouraged by the first breath of criticism. We need not doubt that dogmatism is the prime academic sin in order to recognize that a whiff of it may be valuable in ballasting academic identities. However important rationality may be, it ought not to be allowed an instant and unchallenged dominion of the mind. Intellectual life would be hopelessly unstable if theories were abandoned at the first successful challenge. On the other hand, hard gem-like flames soon burn out, the mastery of a well-developed vocabulary is substituted for thought, and perceptions turn into formulae: these are processes of the human mind, almost as inexorable as the rotation of the seasons. It would certainly be unrealistic to imagine the academic tradition as never anything else but a well-mannered conversation between equals; whether it would be actually illogical to do so is another question altogether.

Whatever happens, universities provide some intellectual guidance, a stock of books, and an opportunity of contemplation to young people who will, if their talents are suitable, profit from it and contribute to it whatever may be the current level of academic vitality judged by other standards. Newman summed these issues up a century ago:

This I conceive to be the advantage of a seat of universal learning, considered as a place of education. An assemblage of learned men, zealous for their own sciences, and rivals of each other, are brought, by familiar intercourse and for the sake of intellectual peace, to adjust together the claims and relations of their respective subjects of investigation. They learn to respect, to consult, to aid each other. Thus is created a pure and clear atmosphere of thought, which the student also breathes, though in his case he only pursues a few sciences out of the multitude. He profits by an intellectual tradition, which is independent of particular teachers, which guides him in his choice of subjects, and duly interprets for him those which he chooses.... A habit of mind is formed which lasts through life, of which the attributes are freedom, equitableness, calmness, moderation, and wisdom; or what in a former Discourse I have ventured to call a philosophical habit. This then I would assign as the special fruit of the education furnished at a University, as contrasted with other places of teaching or modes of teaching.[8]

A philosophical habit: Newman's phrase is deliberately paradoxical. Philosophy is indeed the critic of most things habitual; but philosophy may suitably be reminded that it is itself a habit of mind. Its position in the world may be construed in accordance with the recognition that the thoughts and actions of most human beings most of the time are irredeemably practical. From moment to moment, men are preoccupied with satisfying a ceaseless succession of impulses, some of them so immediate that they issue in a sentence or a gesture, others only to be achieved by the shifts and contrivances of a lifetime. But there are some people who devote part of their time to standing back from all this activity, in order to engage in contemplation.

This activity was regarded by the Greeks as one of the highest options open to human beings. Contemplation covered a large number of possible experiences, but its pursuance was thought to require a good deal of mental energy. This meant that it was comparatively rare in human experience. Contemplation might simply be the capacity to regard the world as if it were a strange and unfamiliar object, thus breaking the habits by which we make ourselves at home in the world. It might issue merely in religious or aesthetic sensations of an agreeable kind – sensations that could be induced by prayers or mantras. But in some people, contemplation became an active and systematic attempt to understand the world we live in. This form of contemplation is philosophy, and universities are its institutional consequences. Newman's view of this activity is interesting, precisely because it sounds old-fashioned and is unaffected by the many distinctions a twentieth-century philosopher would bring to these questions. Each science is, Newman believes, an aspect or abstraction from the whole of knowledge. And what is the activity of these sciences? They 'arrange and

8 *Discourse* V, sec. I, p. 76.

classify facts; they reduce separate phenomena under a common law; they trace effects to a cause. Thus they serve to transfer our knowledge from the custody of memory to the surer and more abiding protection of philosophy, thereby providing both for its spread and its advance.'[9]

As far as it goes, this is a true account of academic procedures, whether they are concerned with engineering or literary criticism. Academic inquiry is a matter of systematization by distinction and connection. But to argue that universities are the impulse to contemplation issuing into a social institution cannot help but suggest one crucial question: once contemplation has become systematic, does it not thereby become one more practical activity amongst others? For it will involve a division of labour, a writing of books, a supplying of references, and it will become the basis of ambitions, since the 'successful' contemplator will soon be accorded a status in the world which will make it, in many respects, indistinguishable from success in commerce, politics and entertainment. The organization of thought will involve an apparatus of technicalities and doctrine which, though it begins in an attempt to understand, can easily come to serve less elevated purposes, such as concealing ignorance and supplying an impressive and impenetrable jargon. Will it not be the case that the universities will generate one more new practical caste of men who, in priestly fashion, base their claim to our attention upon their monopoly of mysteries.

It will, and to some extent it has. Every activity carried on by human beings is, in many respects, practical and requires organization. But the argument of this book is that the university is a good deal more than its practicalities. These practicalities, however, are an important element of its character; and one antidote available to universities against the poison of obscurantism is the undergraduate.

The undergraduate may be specified in the first place in terms of his ignorance. It would be quite wrong, however, to

[9] *Discourse* III, sec. 2, p. 35.

regard this ignorance as a gaping hole to be filled with supplies of information provided by dons. On a sound academic view of what constitutes knowledge, the ignorance of the undergraduate is an active condition which is one of the necessary constituents of an academic tradition. The undergraduate is a Socrates, whose wisdom consists in the fact that he knows he knows nothing. He is therefore a questioner; nor does he stop at a first question, but as an exposition proceeds he must be a continual questioner. Merely by existing he has an influence upon the thinking of academics. But if he actually does his job properly, he will force his teachers to explain their beliefs to him in a language he can understand. It is the undergraduate who tends to impose upon universities simplicity of expression and public availability.

Nearly all intellectual inquiry may be seen as beginning from simple and everyday questions, and developing in time an elaborate superstructure of terms, theories and postulates which render the initial questions unrecognizable. It is often entirely legitimate that this should be so, for the development of a subject means advancing to new questions and abandoning old ones. But the technicalities without which a subject could not develop are also available to conceal real questions and difficulties, and to provide materials whose shuffling may give a delusory appearance of intellectual life where none exists. This was the charge brought against late Scholasticism, and it is a condition commonly found in the social sciences, but few fields of intellectual activity do not succumb to it at times. In the worst cases, the learning of a pompous technical vocabulary is a species of abracadabra by which trivialities are dressed up to look like the latest pronouncements of scientific wisdom. It is the initial business of an undergraduate to limit the scope of this priestly corruption by the active force of his ignorance.

It commonly happens that the graduate student is in a different position; he is often an apprentice who is about to join the corporation himself, and this position may make him the more easily seducible by the current illusions. It is pre-eminently the undergraduate who may live most completely in a kind of social limbo in which self-moving curiosity is freed from the tutelage of childhood and the anxieties of a future career: for it has very commonly been the case that a man's practical training could not begin until he had gone down from the university. Anyone with any familiarity with modern universities will know how very seldom undergraduates actually perform this service. Careerism and a flabby contentment with grasping such externals of a subject as are necessary to pass examinations are very frequent; perhaps they have always been relatively common. But there are always some who play this role; and even the most corrupt undergraduate, the man eager to pretend that he has a grasp of that of which he is actually ignorant, cannot help, by the tasks which his presence involves, going some small way to maintaining academic vitality.

If this view of the undergraduate is accepted, then it follows that there is a certain crudeness about distinguishing the work of universities into teaching and research. Such a distinction has a rough plausibility in the fact that dons spend part of their time lecturing and tutoring, and another part of their time in the operations leading to the books and articles which count as their research: which count, in fact, as a kind of crude measure of 'productivity' in universities. The damage this distinction has done to academic life is to be found in the thousands of trivial and banal papers and reports of research which are published every year. The sad paradox is that contemplation can choke on the products of its own organization.

It is certainly true that teaching and research may be seen as distinct activities, and that each is carried on in a great variety of institutions. The unique character of the university is found nowhere more exactly than in the way it dissolves this distinction. Teaching undergraduates *is*, in part, rethinking the fundamentals of a subject: it constitutes a kind of research. In a properly academic situation, dons would not be tempted, as they are now commonly tempted in many of

71

the actual universities of the world, to regard their students as somewhat dim-witted distractions from the next paper that they hope to produce. It is, of course, true that this fusion of teaching and research is a much more plausible account of some subjects than of others; and it is particularly true in technical subjects that an undergraduate education is barely to be distinguished from a programme of continuous instruction. But this is merely to say that technical subjects, as such, are not academic and only become so as they are seen to involve a higher degree of abstraction than is technically useful.

It follows from this that much of the value to the university of the presence of undergraduates results, paradoxically enough, from the fact that they are in a false position: a university degree is, technically, a licence to teach, and most undergraduates do not intend to teach. This anomaly gives them a detachment from academic preoccupations which allows them to question and probe what they are taught in a way that would not be so easy for an apprentice. It also follows from this that any proposal that university teaching should be directly geared to the practical needs of university students would destroy the valuable role of the undergraduate as a kind of foreign element within the academic world.

In the next section, we shall be considering the logical distinctness of the academic world; but our conclusion here must be that the university ought not to be regarded as the pure flame of rationality burning in the world. It has its social circumstances in medieval society and the Christian religion; but it has also evolved over a long period of time a great number of usages by which the academic tradition is vitally helped to sustain itself against the constant siege of the practical world: the pressure of approximations and 'saving truths'.

4 The Academic and the Practical Worlds

The central argument of this book may be encapsulated in a fable.

Imagine a clan of people who reclaim from the wilderness a large and rambling estate. They live off the garden, breed animals for food, and bequeath what they have achieved to the children. But, above all, they build a large and complex House in which they live and produce things. Each activity – from religion to recreation – sets up a Room of its own in which to grow. Those concerned with the activity of governing claim especially spacious quarters. And in addition to these various Rooms set aside for particular activities, families and individuals manage to build smaller rooms for themselves. Mostly the House is inhabited by vigorous, healthy people who are kept busy by looking after themselves, prosecuting feuds with each other, saving their souls, and keeping themselves distracted. But in the course of generations, a few people appear who like to spend much of their time trying to put together all the beliefs held in the House into one rational belief; or wondering what stars are made of, or what lies beyond the boundaries of the estate, or just poring over old records left by inhabitants now dead and gone.

In time, these people set up a Room of their own, and in

exchange for helping to look after some of the young, they are left more or less undisturbed to pursue their concerns. They organize themselves and their conversations according to different rules from those prevalent in the rest of the House. They are great collectors. They make collections of funny-shaped stones; types of leaves; of the clouds they have seen or the styles of room built they make endless lists and classifications. They accumulate old coins which once were valuable for exchange, but have now been thrown away by all the other inhabitants as no longer of interest because no longer legal tender. Books written in earlier generations to amuse the other inhabitants of the House, but now regarded as tedious and old fashioned (because much of what they refer to has been forgotten), are industriously collected by the inhabitants of what comes to be called the Academic Room. These things are valued, almost perversely as it seems to their fellow-inhabitants, precisely because no one else takes an interest in them. The Academic Room sometimes looks like a kind of intellectual foundlings home, a refuge for orphaned ideas and facts no one else wants to know.

Still, the permission to set up the Academic Room, which looked at the time rather indulgent on the part of the governors, turns out to have been a wise decision. For the inhabitants of the House do recognize the value of writing and reading (skills which it is tedious to acquire, particularly for those who prefer an outdoor life and plenty of exercise) and they are vaguely impressed by the wisdom thought to be contained in a few books surviving from much earlier times. These books are, of course, only accessible to those who have learned the usage of the Academic Room. In time, further, the better class of people in the House got into the habit of sending their children to spend part of their early lives in the Academic Room. Partly, this was just a matter of fashion, and they must all keep up with each other; but partly it came to be recognized that such a period of detachment had some practical advantages. Access of wisdom was thought to accrue to the educated; and there were times when the detachment learned in the Academic Room brought perceptible advantages to the good governing of the House. More than that, the young often came out of the Academic Room capable of seeing things that the other inhabitants had ignored, and they could sometimes bring about startling effects which revolutionized the productive rooms of the House.

The House prospered, enclosed much more ground and built new wings and more specialized outhouses. Many rooms were turned over to educational purposes, but the Academic Room, partly for the extraneous reason that the better class of people tended to go there, never lost its pre-eminence. The result was that, when there came a shakeup in the House and the domestic staff demanded that they should live as well as the better established people, it became a matter of prestige that they too should spend some time in the Academic Room. On the other hand, having got into the Academic Room, many of them could not see much point to it. The conversation was a good deal less racy than what they had been accustomed to, the excitements of passionate commitment were missing, and those old coins and old fashioned books seemed like outmoded junk. The newcomers, being brash and self-confident, attributed this situation not to their own temperamental incomprehension but to senile incompetence on the part of the long-established custodians of the Room. Being accustomed to transform everything into their own image, they demanded a shakeup, so that the Academic Room could take its proper place in the other activities of the House.

Some of them, indeed, went further. They disliked the whole notion of a House organized in terms of Rooms with different rules. They had become addicted to parties, and believed that Rooms merely encouraged an unhealthy furtiveness. Life was only life if everyone lived out in the courtyard in continuous human contact with everyone else.

What this fable suggests is that something valuable would be lost if these changes were to be made. The point of the argument which follows is to specify what that something is. In accordance with the fable, the usage of universities is presented as a 'Room' or 'world' of its own, logically as well as institutionally distinct from other kinds of thought. Academic inquiry is a manner of seeking to understand anything at all, a manner distinguished no doubt by its motives and preoccupations, but distinguished above all by a quite different logic from that of practice. This means that there is a consistent difference in the *kind* of meaning that is found in academic discourse, by contrast with that found in the world at large. To ignore this difference, and to treat universities simply as institutions which provide educational services for society is like treating a Ming vase as a cut glass flower bowl: plausible, but crass. There is an important and neglected sense in which the belief that universities are ivory towers – an image seldom invoked these days without sneer or repudiation – is precisely true. For the purposes of this argument, then, I am asserting a two-world doctrine, and what has to be contested is the view that all knowledge forms a single continuum in which only degrees of obscurity and confusion distinguish the academic from the man in the world. We may for convenience call this – the commonest view of the matter – monism.

A good deal of popularization has taught us to admire the extraordinary growth of knowledge from the time of the 'seventeenth-century revolution' onwards. Our astonishment at our own achievements has been fed by ingenious conjectural statistics, such as the one which claims that the quantity of our knowledge currently doubles about every fifteen years, or that ninety per cent of the scientists who have ever lived are living at this moment. (The actual figures in these claims vary somewhat, as well they might, but there is clearly a lot of popular life left in both notions.) Man is here recognized to be a curious animal who collects bits of knowledge the way the squirrel collects acorns. The moment the cave-dweller had a little leisure from the business of fending off mastodons and spearing supper, he traced out the paths of rivers and tried to make sense of the stars. An important part of this monist picture of human intellectual development is that knowledge and invention went hand in hand, fire and the wheel stimulating man's thought as much as maps and theories transformed his powers. Thousands of nameless martyrs must have died as men acquired a knowledge of what plants were edible and what were poisonous. Such merely empirical accumulations of fact, however, became vastly more powerful once the lore of the priests and (to a much greater extent) the systematization of the philosophers had begun to create an integrated body of knowledge. The growth of knowledge – often interrupted, as often resumed – is the main evidence (dyspeptics would sometimes add, the *only* evidence) for the doctrine of progress. And the doctrine of progress is relevant because it is much the commonest vehicle by which monism has in recent times been carried. For if all knowledge is practical, then it can help us bring about the effects we need. The more knowledge, the more control, until we may even achieve that elusive key to human evolution: the knowledge that will give us the power to control ourselves. One possible consequence of this view of the human situation is that universities become the spearhead of human salvation, and thus the repositories of the faith of many simpler people.

Monism is the belief that there is a single world of facts for man to use, and it may best be seen in intimate association with a set of related doctrine: the doctrine of progress, the theological doctrine that God gave the fruits of the earth to man for his comfort, and the commonsense view that the point of getting to know things is to control them. The discoveries made in universities are commonly thought to be pursued in order that we may cure diseases, improve education, maintain full employment and build better mousetraps. Still, it is clear that universities are different from marketplaces, and even though the monist discounts the difference, he must give some explanation of it. Many commonsense

77

hints are at hand to help him do so. One of the most useful is the distinction between theory and practice. Universities may be seen as dealing with general thoughts which remain sterile until they are united with a purpose and thus give rise to a practical consequence. This movement of theory into the practical world is mediated by the central concept of monism: that of *application*.

Scientific knowledge is 'applied' to the world. The university graduate 'applies' what he has learned: that is to say, he combines it with the practical problem he faces in order to generate a solution. And although there is a great deal that goes on in universities which no one does apply and which it would seem very difficult to apply, there is no doubt that this concept does describe, within its limits, something real. A similar piece of apparatus used to distinguish the practical and the academic spheres is derived from the theory of decision-making: it is the distinction between ends and means. Universities deal primarily with pure theory, and application depends upon ends generated by human desires, which it is no business of the universities to inquire into. For although moral philosophers are sometimes accorded some expert status in the matter of moral ends, an academically trained engineer is no more qualified than the ordinary man to decide which bridges should be built, and where they should be built; and when it comes to making a choice between avoiding unemployment and avoiding inflation, the economist must vacate the expert's platform and step democratically back into the ranks of the citizenry. Finally, this distinction is partnered by a further distinction which, by virtue of its excessive currency amongst undergraduates (who seem to pick it up as toddlers learn to say 'mamma'), has acquired all the enfeebling tedium of something available without hesitation or thought: that between a fact and a value judgement. Science, as conceived monistically, is knowledge organized with all the economy and precision that a system of symbols can supply. All evaluations have been purged from it, for an evaluation either does not raise a question of truth or falsity, or raises it only in an oblique form. By the use of these distinctions all knowledge, from the wisdom of the peasant woman to the hypotheses of the physicist, may be presented as a single continuum which, if distilled out from vagueness, ambiguity and the imponderabilities of human desiring, may be legitimately considered as essentially true or false. And underlying this view of the matter we may always discover the assumption that the only serious reason for seeking to understand things is to control them.

Monism, like all plausible beliefs, may be found both in vulgar and in sophisticated forms, but any expositor will find himself fatally drawn to the vulgar forms because, being suitable for caricature, they create nice clear outlines. Monism expresses very clearly the naive utilitarianism so common among uneducated people – a utilitarianism which takes in not only science (which is the most obviously applicable form of knowledge) but also (for example) history, which is useful because it helps us to understand our 'heritage'. Monists regard history as information revealing who are the people of past times to whom we should be grateful for what we now enjoy. The study of languages is useful in the practical business of helping us get on with foreigners. Classical languages enhance our sense of style and are said to be good training for the mind, while the study of literature is a high-level inquiry into the practical business of cultural enjoyment. Knowledge is thought of as women used to be in times of arranged marriages: some destined to the fertile marriage of application to the world, the rest ending up in the regrettable spinsterdom of the academic journal. Here is a view by which the great achievement of what journalists have called 'the knowledge explosion' will be larger and more comprehensive encyclopedias, in which knowledge is laid out for enjoyment and use. There is a fairly evident continuity between John Stuart Mill's view of knowledge and the patter of the encyclopedia salesman. Monism has the further interest for our argument that it is implied by

79

many socially radical attacks upon the twentieth-century university. Used by radicals, however, it has a special twist: whereas the ordinary monist regards knowledge as a single pool, applied or waiting its turn for application, the radical regards it as a defective pool, from which certain important areas of knowledge are missing because their presence would encourage important political and social changes. On the radical view, the dominant capitalist class in society controls the content of this pool of knowledge so as to ensure that it will not contain anything likely to incite the oppressed to overthrow the present state of society. Consequently the militant can believe that in attacking capitalism and seeking more power within the university he is liberating the academic world from political fetters, and allowing the pool of knowledge to grow more naturally in the future. Indeed, in the Marxist version of monism, theory must always be, in the strictest sense, a reflection of practice, and any other view is taken to be not merely false, but ideological mystification.

Monism, then, is the doctrine that knowledge consists of a vast structure of interlocking facts, varying in their degree of generality and in the extent of their precision, but all describing the same world in exactly the same way. Statements about tables and statements about moving electrons are ultimately translatable one into the other, since both are descriptions of the world in which we live, and any statement about H_2O is not fundamentally different from a statement about water. Monism is, in several versions, an aggressive doctrine, particularly where it becomes a criterion of what is to be regarded as knowledge. In the form of positivism, it asserts not merely that all knowledge is of the same fundamental character, but that that character is most purely exemplified in natural science. This has led on to the attempt to exhibit historical narrative as being fundamentally scientific in its logic. If scientific explanation be always taken as the conjunction in a deductive argument of statements about initial conditions and laws of nature, then the

80

interest of the scientist is in the laws of nature, while that of the historian resides almost exclusively in the initial conditions. Positivism is also dominant in the social sciences where behaviourism, as a criterion of permissible and impermissible evidence, has long been a badge of purity.

Within the universities, monistic beliefs tend to impose upon academic inquiry narrower limits than a straightforward concern for objectivity would otherwise suggest. And although it has long flourished within universities, there are reasons for seeing it as an intellectual rather than an academic belief. It owes a good deal to the Baconian spirit in the seventeenth century, the *philosophes* in the eighteenth, and to radical criticisms of traditional institutions in the nineteenth century. Indeed we may add, somewhat speculatively, that there are some oddities and undercurrents in the mood with which monism has been espoused. For one thing, it often has a religious and messianic look about it, so that it becomes a stick with which to beat lingering survivals of occult thinking or theological presumption. It is almost as if it were a theological doctrine to the effect that God had put men on earth to compile an enormous memorandum of knowledge, and that all the libraries of the world consisted of drafts of this ultimate product. Art is acceptable within this doctrine only as a kind of oblique statement of truths. It has the effect of turning intellectuals into the vanguard of mankind, pressing on over 'the frontiers of knowledge' into the dark and uncharted territories of ignorance. We might even suggest that monism is but one more case of that favourite pastime of modern intellectuals: indulging in fantasies of leadership. Possibly because they had by the nineteenth century grown so numerous, intellectuals began to invent for themselves conceptual 'masses' whom they might lead. Many an intellectual has since made his living out of leading 'the nation'; while many others have led an even more shadowy mass called 'the proletariat'. Positivists cast themselves as the leaders of progressive mankind, and the scourge of superstition, mystification, obscurantism and other intellectual forms of sin. They turned monism (as any doctrine can be turned) into a kind of political melodrama in which they sought to spread knowledge to the ignorant and superstitious masses whose ignorance might be seen, according to taste, as a natural result of the human situation (for every marching army has its stragglers) or as the consequence of scheming priests, kings, aristocrats and other bad men who could more easily dupe the ignorant than the educated.

Much modern enthusiasm for education has been the result of hopeful speculation along these lines. It is clear that the world at large is full of lying, deceit, superstition and self-defeating brutality: men act blindly out of passion rather than far-sightedly out of the understanding which our knowledge can bring. In this way, education has become linked with a great number of idealistic projects. Many people believe that the teaching of science promotes an objective and rational approach to life; while the teaching of classics cannot help, in the view of some teachers of classics, but to dispose a man away from despotism and in favour of liberty and democracy. In these and many other beliefs and projects we may see the mark of monism, of knowledge conceived as *essentially* a single realm.

By contrast with monism, I wish to recommend a dualistic doctrine which asserts a difference of quality between the academic and the practical worlds. The difficulty lies in finding a suitable basis for this distinction. It certainly cannot be based upon intelligence, for there is no doubt that we may find in practical matters the deployment of intelligence on a scale which very commonly dwarfs anything that goes on in universities. Nor can we find such a basis in emphasizing (by a perverse contrast with monism) the very uselessness of most academic discussion, for there would seem to be nothing discussed in universities which might not, in some imaginable circumstances, become useful in practice – if only by the minimal virtue of being a piece of esoteric and precious information likely to make an impression by its very rarity. Context will not help us. We are left facing the somewhat stark question: is the practical utilization of a piece of information merely an accident (as the monist would hold) or does it somehow affect the very meaning and significance of the information?

The first observation to be made about practical beliefs would seem to be that a great number of them are false. Sometimes this falsity is important in practice – as when I spoon into my coffee a white substance I have taken to be sugar but which is, in fact, arsenic. But a great many false beliefs are just as useful as true beliefs. I can navigate my way about the globe on the assumption that the earth is flat. Faith healers cure many people of diseases which they certainly do not understand except in a very primitive way. And a great many cures of mental illnesses are effected by a body of psychiatrists who hold mutually contradictory doctrines of the nature of the mind and the illnesses that affect it. It is further the case that we are all, in practical life, environed by things that we would rather not know, and by beliefs which we choose for reasons quite other than a concern with truth: religious beliefs, for example, or the beliefs we hold because each of us is the centre of our own small world, and seeks to keep control of what may be admitted to this world. It is a truth now much canvassed among philosophers of science that there is no theory, no matter how dotty, which will not provide confirmations. From anti-semitism to astrology, confirming instances come cheap; all kinds of inconclusive-nesses of evidence are seized upon, in the thinking of the practical world, to sustain what is in many cases nothing more substantial than the belief that we *wish* to hold.

This suggests an initial basis for our distinction: in the academic world, the only relevant criterion is that of truth or falsity; in practice, on the other hand, the criterion may be summed up in portmanteau fashion as effectiveness. Truth is very frequently a part of effectiveness, but by no means the only part (or indeed, in many cases, the main part). In practice, it is often worthwhile to judge a statement as mean or generous, consoling or hurtful, reactionary or progressive, helpful or harmful: academically speaking, such things are irrelevant. If this is so, then there will be many circumstances in which it will be beside the point – 'academic' is the word commonly used – to spend time arguing about the falsity of a belief which obviously serves us perfectly well.

Now a monist, confronted with this kind of argument, would concede the point with some impatience. There are indeed false beliefs (he might concede) which will produce a required effect, but they are always second best. There is always a true belief which would produce the same effect; and further, a false belief is likely to let people down when the circumstances change. Modern astronomy may not be much better than Ptolemaic for a limited bit of navigation in the Mediterranean, but it can produce a vastly greater number of intended effects than its more primitive competitors. And while faith healers do produce some inexplicable successes, their general rate of success is vastly less than that of modern doctors: further, their practical effectiveness is restricted precisely by the fact that they have so little understanding of the reality of what they are doing. This means that their skill is something static, and incapable of the cooperative development possible to modern scientific medicine. Truth, our monist would conclude, is always the fundamental test of belief.

A good deal of this may be admitted, for it is certainly true that the truth of beliefs is very frequently of practical value. This is a difficult question, and it is rendered all the more difficult by an attitude we all commonly adopt when considering it. For in thinking of cases such as that in which a person continues smoking by blotting out of his mind the evidence connecting lung cancer and smoking, we often feel that the more truth or reality there is in people's behaviour the better. Whole artistic genres are devoted to charting the miseries of those people who are 'living a lie' and to the exhilaration and nobility which results from the moment when the falsities of their lives collapse into a climax, after which protagonist and reality live happily ever after. Vast areas of life are obviously built upon deception: upon *suppressio veri* and *suggestio falsi*. Industries, like advertising and public relations, perhaps even politics, may be plausibly seen as resting upon deceit. In a perfect world – in heaven, or the classless society, according to choice – such things would no doubt disappear, and we might all lead lives of such transparency that even privacy, the evident medium in which falsities and furtivenesses thrive, would disappear forever. Here then is a moral doctrine, loosely linked to what we have called monism, which suggests that we would all be better off if the element of falsity in practical life disappeared altogether.

In order to deal with this, we need to show that there are some elements of falsity in practical life which are necessary and cannot conceivably be removed. And it is certainly the case that there is very frequently no *available* true belief on which to act. Politicians, spies and fugitives, for example, usually assume that no one is to be trusted, and this is usually false. But the true belief (that *some* people are not to be trusted) would be of little use. Hence there is at least one kind of systematic error in some practical activities – that which comes from erring on the safe side.

A further class of useful errors is constituted of those false beliefs without which we should not act at all. The human situation is such that a good deal of essential information is concealed from us because it has not yet happened: politics and marriage, the investment of money and the building of houses, not to mention the declaration of war, are among the things which sometimes lead people into saying: 'If only I had known what I was letting myself in for, I should never have started.' Without this human propensity to act upon inadequate or quite false information, human life would be vastly different. There are also times when the false belief is the product of the passion of the present moment: a little rational reflection would bring home to anyone that a crucial belief on which an action depends is false, but the moment for that rational reflection has not yet come. Any number of heroic acts are performed in the belief that the bullet won't hit me, or that the collective act of heroism performed by our unit, or our class, or our contemporaries, will shine imperishably in the annals of humanity. Most such beliefs are false, and posterity is too busy living its own imperishable moments to have much time for saving the moments of most of its ancestors from perishing. Human beings, as the poet said, and as we hardly need telling in this century, can bear very little reality.

These considerations suggest to us that one of the primary distinctions between the academic and the practical worlds rests upon the simplest and most luminous of facts: that in a university, no one has to come to a conclusion upon which a decision must be based. A don can afford the luxury of allowing the evidence to dictate quite precisely what conclusion he will come to, and dons do, in fact, spend a great deal of their time explaining the reasons why nothing very substantial in the way of conclusions is possible. Further, even if he does come to a conclusion, any academic will soon find that it has not been locked away in the monist's grand encyclopedia as another bit of knowledge in humanity's upward climb, but that it sits astride an unstable mass of evidence which new young dons are likely to revise. In the academic world, conclusions simmer together with the evidence, and there is no point at which they can ever be detached from it. In the practical world, on the other hand, conclusions often long outlive the evidence for them. Decisions have to be taken and minds made up. This must generally be done on what are, in academic terms, inadequate grounds. There is about the taking of decisions in the practical world an irredeemable element of improvization which renders it necessarily, not contingently, subject to error. And it is the vast achievement of establishing universities as institutions to have created conditions of life in which this constant practical pressure towards the botched or best available conclusion has been neutralized.

We have so far developed this argument with a rather simple-minded conception of truth: we have taken it to be a matter of propositions which correspond or do not correspond to the facts. A good deal of the plausibility of arguments on all philosophical questions depends upon the examples chosen. We are led in rather different directions according as we focus our minds either on 'Napoleon died in 1821' and 'water boils at 100 degrees centigrade at sea level' on the one hand, or the Heisenberg uncertainty principle or the destructiveness of the Thirty Years War on the other. In practical life, we settle for concepts which are 'near enough' and it is pedantic to make them any more precise. Practical discourse is made up of categories like 'friend', 'enemy', '£10 tenant', 'communist', 'good to eat', 'ripe for revolution' and the like. These are notions riddled with imprecision and often dependent upon variations of personal taste. Practical concepts frequently combine a description with an attitude towards the thing described. Furthermore, these distinctions – the way in which the infinitely divisible fabric of reality is grasped – depend upon our interests and our passions, or, in the more pompous terminology currently fashionable, upon our social and cultural orientation. Different cultures and times, different categories; and this instability is intensified by an incessant responsiveness to changing circumstances. But clearly such semantic circumstances are not suitable to the growth of science, and the problem which immediately arises is the following: is it the case that technical terminology is to practical language what surgery is to butchery? Or is it rather that the development of understanding steadily produces more serious asymmetrics between the academic and the practical than merely degree of precision?

This is clearly one of the central questions of philosophy. It is the question answered in Platonic terms by the distinction between the unstable opinion of the practical world, *doxa,* and the reasoned and organized concepts which made up what Plato called *episteme.* The distinction between a theory and a model, and the relation of both to what they purport to explain, is a modern version of similar preoccupations. Our concern is a limited one, and the view I wish to support is that the result of academic inquiry into anything is to produce an entity different in kind from the practical concept with which the inquiry began. A historian like Professor Holt begins with one Magna Carta, the ancestor of civil rights, and ends up with a view of the complicated events of the thirteenth century so very different from the popular legend that we may legitimately regard it as a different thing altogether. A scientist, starting with the projectiles which are fired from cannons, ends up with an elaborate theory of the mathematics of curves. The literary historian who, as a child, read *Gulliver's Travels* as an adventure story, uncovers a political and allegoric content by looking more closely at it in relation to Swift's life and the history of the period in which he lived. It is a common popular belief, prevalent in the practical world, to regard as 'the same thing' whatever has the same name, and to regard all such 'names' as if they were fundamentally descriptions of the real world. This tendency gives rise to the type of popular paradox typified by such statements as that a table is 'really' just a swarm of electrons. On the argument I am presenting, the world is very much more complicated and varied than this popular view would suggest, and there are very much more complicated relations between 'theory' and 'the world' than those of description. Indeed, a great deal of what must academically be regarded as the 'nonsense of the practical world' arises from taking as straightforward description academic constructions which have a much more oblique relation to what we think we see and hear. Here, in the illusion that all theory ultimately describes, we may find the epistemology upon which the monist's key concept of 'application' rests – whatever does not fit this theory must be relegated to an inferior realm: fantasy, nonsense, advocacy or justification. It is this inferior realm which is populated with the logical *untermenschen* known as value judgements.

Monism is wrong in suggesting that the only relations between academic theory and what may popularly be called 'the real world' are those of description and application. When practical entities are taken up by academics they evolve into quite different things: they belong now in propositions which are fundamentally hypothetical and subject to ceaseless modification; they may be challenged and changed according to rules of manipulation different from those of practice, and the result is that they no longer fit the practical world. A similar change happens with the reverse traffic of academic materials being taken over for use in the practical world. Such a transfer is always merely of fragmentary parts of the academic world. The academically hypothetical becomes the technologically assumed, and the academic giving practical advice turns into a completely different kind of figure called an 'expert'. Politicians are prone to ransack books of anthropology for statements which appear to support the political position they have already taken up on the race question. Plato's notion of the philosopher king is from its author's text untimely ripp'd to support the pretensions of some ambitious elite. But thus severed, these notions resemble the coral in tropical seas, full of colour and fascination in the water, but grey and dull out of it. These are simply two kinds of adventures that may happen to ideas – in the one case, a movement towards understanding, in the other, a use for the purpose of changing the world or, what at this level of abstraction is the same thing, the prevention of change.

It is significant to note that the uses made of academic ideas in the practical world are not academically corrigible. A politician who has just made a successful use of the legend of Magna Carta in a political speech is unlikely to be very concerned if an academic comes up to him later to explain that that famous document signified something very different from the guarantee of civil liberty which had featured in the politician's speech. What interests the politician is the fact that Magna Carta is (marginally) still extant on the statute books, and that everyone in his audience will be familiar with a melodrama in which King John features as a bad king brought to book by (more or less) liberty-loving barons. An American politician in similar circumstances may well use Patrick Henry's famous statement: 'Give me liberty or give me death!' In both cases, the practical use of these historical reminiscences takes for granted that King John, the barons, and Patrick Henry were people like us, and meant the same thing by the same words. Rap Brown, in providing a Black version of this particular bit of the American legend: 'I say to America: Fuck it. Freedom or Death!', takes the legend for granted. A historian, on the other hand, will end up by treating such legends as Hollywood History: the belief that the past consists of men like us, in fancy dress.[1] And the more the historian washes our twentieth-century preoccupations out of the legend, in order to discover in its own context what was meant (in our examples) by liberty, and what was involved in the demand for judgement by peers, the less these episodes, as historically understood, have to do with the conflicts of the present time. But it is clear that in investigating these historical events and there-fore, it might seem, destroying the legend, the historian is in no way attacking liberty or civil rights. The most plausible conclusion, then, would seem to be that the Magna Carta of legend is a quite different thing from the Magna Carta of the twelfth-century historian, a difference masked, as so often, by the fact that the same name covers both. And the situa-tion grows even more complicated if we bring in the idea of Magna Carta as it affected English political ideas in the seventeenth century – an idea different from both those we have considered. In the case of a name like 'the Battle of the Boyne' we find a variety of both practical and historical events. Now it is perfectly possible to insist, with brutalist common sense, that these are simply different versions or interpretations of 'the same things'; but when it is impossible

[1] Intellectual historians, following Professor Butterfield, commonly refer to such legends as 'Whig History'.

to give any account of that 'same thing' which is not also an interpretation; and when the logic of the concept as it appears in practical and in academic contexts is quite different, then it is difficult to see what is gained by this insistence on the misleadingly obvious. What is achieved is to make us the dupes of the unreflective monism embedded in some of our linguistic practices.

Our intellectual situation would appear to be such, then, that we are faced with a dilemma. For in the case of Magna Carta we find that the politician cannot use the concept unless it is anachronistic, while the historian cannot use it if it is. More generally, we have the alternative of being academic and ineffective (or irrelevant, as the term goes today) or, alternatively, practical and if not false at least unacademic. Here is a fork which, while commonly recognized in all the pejorative uses of the word 'academic', is nevertheless concealed from us by the fact that language contains vastly fewer names than concepts. Further, it would simply be a misunderstanding on his part if our monist were to counter this argument by asserting that the more truth there is in the teaching of history the better, since history has often been used in the past to reinforce unpleasantly nationalist or racialist emotions. For it is clear that what the monist seeks in this respect is not 'real history' (which teaches nothing practical to anyone) but a history seeming to encourage different moral opinions: less of 'Death to the French!' and more of 'Kameradschaft'. This may well be desirable, but it is certainly not the replacement of 'false' history by true.

The cognitive dilemma, by which we are faced with a choice between being academic and ineffective, or practical and effective, makes it clear that universities must be accounted a vast and unlikely achievement. For the constant pressure of practice is such that only a set of most unusual contingencies occurring together could possibly have permitted such an institution to come into existence and to entrench itself in such organizational ways as to survive for centuries. And the paradoxical result has been, of course, an enormous boost in practical power; for the world happens to be the sort of place in which the free movement of disinterested inquiry allows the mind to arrive at places which suggest practical expedients which could not be directly approached. It required monastic attitudes, a tradition of corporate association deriving from the politics of Europe, an enthusiasm for a past culture, not to mention the resourcefulness of concrete individuals, to bring universities into existence. And as one of the remoter consequences of their durability we may cite the infinite patience and skill with which archaeologists dig to recapture not treasure, but the lost past of mankind – one of the many ways in which the academic tradition has given to Western civilization a unique place in the achievements of mankind.

It might seem that, in using historical examples, I have been choosing particularly favourable ground for the argument I wish to present. It will be argued that in technology we do find a precise example of academic propositions being applied. But this would not be true. Science consists of a vast structure of hypotheses, with a good deal of interlocking, which scientists both develop by logic and imagination, and test by experiment. It is an ever-changing world in which those theories which are currently accepted must be assumed liable to revision in the light of future work. Although we do, of course, recognize that 'in practice' many things have been 'scientifically proven', this is in strict terms a vulgar expression, since proof is only properly applicable to logic and mathematics (and in a different sense, law) while scientific hypotheses may have strong support but can never be regarded as necessary truths. No part of science can safely be regarded as beyond revision, if for no other reason than that each part is affected by the changing context in which it must always be construed. And while scientists do often make confident judgements about what they think is indubitable, they are also prone in their general behaviour to recognize just this kind of tentativeness. But this view of science is not, of course, the view taken in unsophisticated writing. The vulgar opinion is that science is a glare of findings surrounded by a penumbra of doubtful hypotheses, and scientists, like men clearing a field, steadily produce greater numbers of increasingly reliable propositions. Now if we inquire how it is that so erroneous a view of science has become so current, the answer in our terms is perfectly clear: the general public have mistaken for science a set of propositions which (though often identical in notation) are essentially practical. As with Magna Carta, two things have been taken to be one. In the case of science, tentative propositions logically and experimentally linked to other assertions similarly tentative, have been confused with the assertions – isolated from a context of inquiry and regarded as certain – which serve as the basis for action. The Western World has seen a succession of cosmologies in which the system of Ptolemy was superseded by that of Newton, and that of Newton by Einstein. But popular opinion has taken each in turn as the final pronouncement of science, popularizers have developed 'philosophies' on the same assumption, and practical men have produced effects, often very complex and successful effects, by taking for granted this or that fragment of a complex scientific system. In other words, an apparently scientific proposition when used in technology must be construed differently: it is taken as certain (which it cannot be in science) and it is sundered from a much more complex system in association with which it is scientifically to be understood.

The situation is the same, let it be added, in philosophy, which provides a special kind of rational explanation of the world we live in, but does not, and cannot, legislate about our practical concerns. If it appears to do so, then we may be certain that the legislation is not philosophy, even though it may superficially resemble it in verbal construction. Aristotle, for example, argued in the *Politics* that some men are by nature slaves, and this scandalous opinion has provoked a good deal of unease among his liberal commentators. It has vulgarly been taken as Aristotle's 'justification' of the

Athenian practice. But Aristotle is simply saying that the
common practice of slavery is not rationally inexplicable, and
that some people are more suited to obedience than others.
But what he does not say, and could not philosophically say,
is that in any particular society men ought to institute
slavery legally. There is no logical contradiction in accepting
Aristotle's argument on slavery and supporting political
democracy – indeed there are respects in which Aristotle did
this himself.

The distinction between the practical and the academic
worlds is exemplified in the difference between a phrase book
and a grammar book. Phrase books are quick and effective,
and they are based upon what experience shows to be the
most commonly used words and idioms. To master a phrase
book is to learn a language after the manner in which a child
learns it. And as this example shows, it is by no means the
case that someone who has mastered a phrase book is limited
to the mechanical repetition of phrases about the pen of my
aunt and the demeanour of the coachman. A little ingenuity
will generate an infinite number of further possible sentences
out of the phrase book, according to the skill of the user. A
grammar book, on the other hand, is an analysis of the
language, and the fact that grammar is not central to speaking is shown by the fact that it is taught to children who
already have a fluent mastery of their language. Thereby
they learn not to do the right thing, but to know why it is the
right thing. A grammar book begins, of course, as a description and analysis of an actually spoken language, but in time
it comes to act as a criterion of how that language ought to be
spoken. It is often the case that to learn grammar is the
soundest and most reliable way of learning a language; but
there are other ways of doing so, and it is not uncommon to
find someone who has an excellent mastery of the grammar
but has difficulty in making himself understood. Further, an
understanding of grammar, though it is slow and indirect,
eventually supplies a mastery of the language, along with its
past and its possibilities, which cannot be found in the

phrase book. Phrase books depend upon current practice, and therefore go out of date very quickly. Each has its advantages, each its limitations. But the grammar book, in being the paradigm of a form of learning which has its own inherent order and rationality independent of relevance and usage, exemplifies the education of the schools, while the phrase book which is responsive to what pupils wish to learn and to what is currently going on in society, is equally the paradigm of that useful learning to which we must all devote so much of our time.

There is obviously a good deal of traffic between the academic and the practical worlds: they are, after all, merely abstractions, and any academic will imaginatively participate in both. But as a proposition moves from the one world to the other, it will suffer certain significant changes. An academic theory will lose its hypothetical character and turn into a practical assumption: something taken for granted. A philosophical argument (which is a form of explanation) will turn into a justification (whose business is to defend, not to explain). Practical concepts are vague, fluid and at the mercy of their connotation; but they appear in propositions generally much more dogmatically asserted than in the academic world. Academic discourse, by contrast, tends to dissolve concepts into simpler and harder entities which may be more playfully entertained. To wonder about a concept, which is a form of playing with it, is one of the commonest gates from the one world into the other. Most beliefs are, as it were, locked firmly into place and pinned down by the practical purposes they serve. And what is irrelevant to these purposes is, by practical men, correctly dismissed as 'academic'. Everything academic began its life in the practical world, however remotely; and from the academic world, by a process of simplification, comes a stream of suggestions, assumptions, ideas to be used and abused, manners of viewing problems, and a host of other things which are indeed useful, but not in the direct form of 'application' imagined by the monist. Understanding and control must be recognized as different kinds of human activity. An interest in control focuses our mind upon what is relevant to the purpose we have in hand, while he who understands is able to follow the contours of the world as it is with a freedom unknown to the man who seeks control. We have already seen that the academic world grew out of religion, and religion very commonly adopts an attitude of piety towards at least some parts of the world. To try to control or manipulate (certain aspects of) God's handiwork is an impiety. The academic world would seem to have inherited this kind of piety with regard to everything that exists. It renounces passionate involvement, as did its monkish ancestors, and gets in return a freedom to roam wherever its inclination leads.

It should be clear from this argument that any distinction between the academic and the practical world in terms of fact and value is blind to certain crucial features of our knowledge. It is certainly true that evaluation is a practical business; but the practical world includes also the vast descriptive apparatus by which we make our way in the world. The moment a practical purpose lights up the world, what is illuminated has a different character from what the academic studies: we are back in Plato's cave. The most easily accessible logic of practice is that which has been studied since the time of the Sophists as rhetoric, for in the behaviour of speakers before courts and political assemblies we may observe a logical design which is too conspicuously directed towards the end of persuasion to be mistaken for scientific inquiry. But to concentrate our attention upon rhetoric is to notice only a small part of practice. A very large number of the beliefs we espouse are designed not to contribute to discovery, but to identify ourselves (both to ourselves and others) as members of some admirable moral class. The membership of such moral classes is not at all a hypothesis which we seriously are prepared to discuss in terms of the evidence available. We commonly formulate the moral class in such a way as to protect ourselves from evidence that might refute, and we are constantly aware of confirming, instances. Furthermore, should anyone choose to deny the moral identification we have made, it is very seldom the result of a disinterested passion, but commonly in response to some practical impulse of his own. Practical discourse is full of vagueness, vacuity, 'metaphysical' elevation, dogmatism (the logical form of shouting) and equivocation: and it is difficult to see how else people could carry on – even though precisely these devices may also be recognized as leading people into unhappiness. Philosophers of science these days commonly distinguish scientific theories from other kinds of intellectual production in terms of refutability. This is a logical criterion : but it may also plausibly be seen as a moral one. For it demands that the framer of scientific (and indeed any kind of academic) hypotheses is under an obligation to take the risk of being refuted by the evidence. He must not take refuge in the 'monster-barring' and 'concept-stretching' stratagems by which we all defend ourselves in practical life.[2] This has tempted some expositors of the academic world into the belief that it is *morally* distinct from – indeed, superior to – the practical : that in the practical world, men seek the security of moral commitment and entrench themselves behind absolutes, while the academic adventures freely wherever the evidence may take him. What academic could fail to be tempted by such an opinion? He is so often presented as belonging to a class of sedentary and prudent men that the opportunity to appear as a hero is not to be lightly brushed aside. Nevertheless, it should be remembered that the advancing of theories has its practical side, and that an academic who has advanced a hypothesis has sunk a certain amount of his identity into it. In such situations, every academic becomes familiar with the stratagems of moral trench-warfare.

For so long as we fail to recognize the duality of the academic and the practical worlds, we shall connive at a

[2] Stratagems described by Professor Imre Lakatos, *Criticism and the Growth of Knowledge*, London 1970.

situation in which each bullies the other. The practical man has his own criteria of what is worth doing, and seeks from academics whatever may help him in his designs; monism is current in part because it is necessary to facilitate this kind of bullying. On the other hand, academics – or rather those familiar with the academic world who are in love with reason and are therefore often called rationalists – tend to believe that any human activity which is not the outcome of an explicit theory must be the result of blind impulse, and can only be improved if it is superseded by a 'theory' of its own. Graduates often come down from universities filled with a missionary zeal to see the standards of objectivity and impartiality they have learned at the university transform the world.

Still, there is no doubt that it is practicability which seeks to subdue the academic world, while any appearance to the contrary must be seen as a form of practicality using the occasionally influential garb of learning. Since it is a characteristic of the academic world to be blind to the practicalities of its own survival – indeed, to any practicalities at all – practical men can subdue the academic world by infecting it with their own sense of urgency. For urgency is the demand that a conclusion must be arrived at within a limited time, and is an infallible indicator of practical concerns. Urgency has often influenced academic preoccupations by means of a confusion between two kinds of 'problem', one practical, and the other academic.

Everyone is familiar with a collection of 'World Problems' or 'Great Issues of Our Time' which circulate like punch-drunk boxers through the magazine sections of the quality press; world population increase, the effect of chemicals upon the balance of nature, world government, pollution, the two cultures and the affluence gap are current examples. All of these, being practical problems, are of no academic interest whatsoever. The reason why world population is going up very fast is no mystery at all; nor is there any mystery about some of the conditions which would slow it down. The only difficulty is the entirely practical matter of how to bring some sufficient set of these conditions about, and it is only a problem for people who are interested in trying to do so. If there are interesting academic problems, they will be about genetics, or human behaviour, and thus only tangentially related to such a world problem as the 'population explosion'.

This particular implication of the distinction I am recommending will seem paradoxical to some readers and outrageous to others. For, it will be said, any of these problems might in time lead to the disappearance of human life from the earth; at the very least to its violent impoverishment. What will then become of universities? The answer is, no doubt, that if these predictions are correct then universities will disappear along with everything else human. The point, however, is that the survival of universities is not an academic concern of universities. It is, of course, an important practical concern, and it deserves attention in practical terms. But such practical responsibility does not exist in the academic world. That is indeed precisely one of its greatest attractions.

The fact that a problem is urgent, then, will be the clearest sign we can have that it is a practical problem; and as a practical problem it will be quite distinct from an academic one. Medically, the problem of cancer is two problems : a practical problem because we all want to cure the thousands who die of the disease, and a medical problem – or, rather, cluster of problems – about the behaviour of cells. It happens in this case that a solution to the academic problem may be a precondition of a solution to the practical problem : at least, this is a plausible way of looking at it. It might happen, of course, that someone might stumble across a cure for cancer, highly effective but quite mysterious. Or research might discover an explanation that did not help in curing. In the case of a cure without understanding, the practical problem would virtually have ceased, except perhaps for a certain amount of residual anxiety that the cures might merely be flukes, and that until the academic problem had been solved

– i.e., until doctors worked out some idea of *why* the cure was a cure – then there would be a considerable possibility of relapse. It seems very commonly to happen in our civilization that practical problems and academic problems are to be found in clusters, and that academics may legitimately employ huge research facilities in groping with academic problems on which hinge practical matters of great weight. This has often been a fortunate circumstance for academics, as it means that social and financial support is available for what otherwise would have had to be left to one side. But it is an unfortunate circumstance in that it often leads academics to become merely research agents of practical concerns like the government, with the consequence that the coherence of academic work is impaired by the intrusion of practical concerns.

The remoteness of academic from practical concerns must be regarded not as a surviving tradition from less enlightened days, but an essential condition of the maintenance of the academic world. The practical world is one we cannot help living in, but the academic world requires special cultivation, and did not come into existence in any significant form until quite recent times. And the condition of its survival is that it should be isolated from the essentially practical task of taking decisions. In the world of practical responsibilities decisions must be taken; and if there isn't enough information for a sound decision, then a decision is risked and the fingers are crossed. But the essential concern of the academic world is with the cogency of evidence: what the evidence will suggest and what the evidence will support. Academics are, as a matter of fact, frequently turning away from the substantial issue of their discussion to consider just how far they are entitled by what they know to arrive at a conclusion. This habit of mind is peculiarly irritating if urgent questions are at stake.

It might seem that the argument that I am presenting is simply the recommendation of a remote ideal, having no connection either with what happens or with what is possible. There is certainly plenty of discussion suggesting that universities must modernize themselves and play their 'proper' part in society. Such discussion might persuade some readers that my description of the academic world is, if possibly desirable in some vague way, nonetheless entirely out of touch with modern realities. All that needs to be said here is that I am describing the character of a good deal of the work which is actually carried on in universities today. Much else, of course, happens in universities, much of it practical. It is exactly this 'much else' which is threatening to transform the academic world. Universities find themselves subject to government pressures and to demands that their research facilities be used in cooperation with industry. Student militants exert another kind of practical pressure. Each of these unacademic groups wants to change the universities, and each of them presents what it wants as if it were reform. Meanwhile, dons themselves are weakened by the lure of money, fame and power: all practical objectives and mightily desirable.

Some element of compromise on these matters seems eminently possible. The people who live in the academic world are, in addition to being dons, also citizens, fathers, mortgagees: they play most of the parts of modern men. It has recently been much less the case that universities are places of refuge for suitable men of a wayward, eccentric and wondering disposition. Further, it is perfectly possible for some academics to live happily in both worlds – capable of bringing their intellectual skills to bear on practical tasks without allowing this to begin colouring their vision of their academic work. But it takes a clear head, not to mention talents not universal in the human race, to do this. Above all, there is abundant room in the modern world for both teaching and research in practical matters which need not pretend to the name of 'university'. The attempt to dress up all tertiary educational activities in academic trimmings is no more than an expensive piece of vulgarity.

And here in this matter of prestige lies one crux of the

matter. It happens to be the case that, for reasons partly extraneous to its academic functions, the universities have come to be regarded as the apex of advanced education. Consequently everyone wants to share in a university education, and many are commonly disappointed with what they find. It cannot be too highly emphasized that the distinction between the academic and the practical worlds is not a matter of status. It would be absurd to say that either was superior to the other. The only person who would try and say so would be someone who imagined that the academic world was fine and spiritual, while the practical world was vulgar and materialistic. Such a view would be a total misunderstanding of the distinction I am advancing. The practical world as I have presented it is not simply a place for supplying the material necessities of civilization; it includes, as well, man's preoccupation with the salvation of his soul, and the survival of humanity as well as the values of love and friendship.

Here then is a restatement of a common distinction between the academic and the practical worlds, a distinction which is embodied in the popular attitudes that recognize that academics are very commonly inferior practitioners, and that young men straight down from the universities, with theory pouring out of their ears, have a great deal of unlearning to do before they can become effective doctors, engineers or businessmen. It is a distinction which has to be made, now, in elaborate terms. For on my reading of the situation, the Academic Room in the House has become crowded with a new collection of people who do not quite understand what the point of the Room is. They are half impressed by what they have found, but a little baffled also. It is as if they had taken diamonds of thought for bits of shiny glass, and classical texts for yesterday's weekend reviews. They believe that the Room is out of date and in need of a shakeup. If they get their way, they will have made the Academic Room indistinguishable from the rest of the House.

Part Two
Imitations of the Academic

5 The Battle of Beliefs

The distinction between the academic and the practical world has become obscured in recent times by an extraordinary situation with which we are so familiar that we no longer see its oddity. Yet it was very clearly diagnosed more than a century ago by Newman:

An intellectual man, as the world now conceives of him, is one who is full of 'views' on all subjects of philosophy, on all matters of the day. It is almost thought a disgrace not to have a view at a moment's notice on any question from the Personal Advent to the cholera or mesmerism. This is owing in great measure to the necessities of periodical literature, now so much in request. Every quarter of a year, every month, every day, there must be a supply, for the gratification of the public, of new and luminous theories on the subjects of religion, foreign politics, home politics, civil economy, finance, trade, agriculture, emigration, and the colonies. Slavery, the gold-fields, German philosophy, the French Empire, Wellington. Peel, Ireland, must all be practised on, day after day, by what are called original thinkers. As the great man's guest must produce his good stories or songs at the evening banquet, as the platform orator exhibits his telling facts at midday, so the journalist lies under the stern obligation of extemporising his lucid views, leading ideas, and nutshell truths for the breakfast table.[1]

[1] Newman, *op. cit.*, preface.

A diffused and weakened intellectuality, far more pretentious than the earlier spread of literacy, now dominates European awareness. It is visible in our addiction to intellectual journalism and to ideologies, both of which we shall presently discuss; but its primary root lies in our addiction to general beliefs. And it is the generality of the beliefs which is difficult to understand. Why, for example, in a society in which a woman may at her choice get married or take a job, should anyone care passionately to debate the *general* proposition that a woman's place is in the home? Or again, in an entirely liberal society, where authority takes virtually no interest in sexual mores, why should anyone care about the *general* question of pre-maritial sex? And while it is very easy to see why people should care very strongly to establish that membership of a racial class should have no bearing upon citizenship rights, it is not at all easy to see why anyone should bother to assert that this or that race is superior to, inferior to, or indeed equal to any other race. What evidence could be seriously adduced in favour of any of these propositions, even upon the charitable assumption that their meaning could be elucidated with any clarity? In all such cases, the generality of the questions renders the conclusions valueless. They are questions where individual variation is sovereign, and this has been legally recognized in that liberal societies leave the practical aspect of most such decisions to individual choice.

Some of these liberties are so remote in time that we imagine them immemorial: as in the freedom people have to wear whatever clothes they choose – a freedom which in the seventeenth century had to be asserted against demands that the lower classes should be forced to continue wearing hose rather than ape the fashions of their betters. Other liberties, such as the full removal of legal restrictions upon women, are more recent. In so liberal a situation, one might imagine that the continued assertion of general beliefs about how individuals should behave would be indistinguishable from impertinence. Far from it. The processing of beliefs has turned into an industry whose business it is to maximize the production of insignificant opinion.

This industry, with its roots in newspapers and broadcasting, rests upon one of the most powerful moral attitudes of modern society: that to have a lot of general beliefs in one's head is admirable, to be deficient in them contemptible. A man may be stupid, aggressive and insanitary, but if he has beliefs, and better still, if he 'stands up for' his beliefs, then he can't be all bad. The tradition of pseudo-intellectuality which recommends that people should 'think for themselves' concerns itself not with academic illumination but with an abundance of these general beliefs. The agnostic who makes the Socratic response to the pollster's questions is regularly heaped with scorn as one too pusillanimous to play the game. Yet since the questions are foolish, the believers don't know what they are talking about, and the questions mostly of a kind which it is logically impossible should generate any sensible conclusion, the man who replies 'I don't know' when asked his opinion of the performance of governments, the best kind of educational system, the economic condition of the country, the current state of its morals, the political behaviour of foreign government, and the other familiar bits of the pollster's equipment – such a man ought to be regarded as a model of integrity. We accord admiration instead to the garrulous feather-wit with the positive opinions.

Why has this curious situation come about? Many of the reasons are not far to seek. Newman pointed to one of them in saying that to have opinions is to appear an educated man. It is to proclaim the fruits of one's thought, and to be thoughtful is to possess a virtue. Successful thought issues in conclusions, and the adoption of a general belief permits the appearance of having thought things through to a conclusion, without very much ratiocinative effort having been expended. A further cause of addiction to general beliefs is the growth of democratic sentiments. A persistent thread in the European tradition identifies true humanity with political engagement. In recent centuries, this belief has appeared as the right of all citizens to vote. And in the liberal form of democracy which became current in the nineteenth century, voting was imagined to be a judgement which followed thought about general issues. This view of voting is plausible because it makes the voter a kind of remote participant in a deliberative assembly, and assemblies do indeed discuss issues in terms of general beliefs and circumstantial detail. The theory of rhetoric is a good account of the behaviour of political assemblies, but it has turned out to be a bad guide to the nature of voting. When it was realized that most votes are actually cast upon the basis of traditional allegiances, party loyalty, upon reaction to personalities and upon feel for the current political situation, liberal commentators were cast into gloom. For it seemed to put politics at the mercy of irrationality. The educated, who were by and large liberally inclined, thought that the solution was to inject issues of general belief into political education, and schools were encouraged to teach civics and current affairs conceived in this controversial way. Whatever value such attempts may have, they cannot convincingly be presented as an improvement of political standards. For popular judgement on many general issues is often unintelligent, whereas popular judgement as to changes in the holding of power and which party can be trusted is much less vulnerable to this kind of criticism. The success or failure of democracy rests upon quite other grounds than the articulateness and intellectuality of voters. But the contrary view is a powerful cause of our preoccupation with general beliefs.

Such are some of the obvious and familiar reasons for the modern passion for believing. Beneath reasons of this type lie much more fundamental features of our society. For the point of holding a belief is to identify oneself as a certain type of person: the business of general beliefs is to identify the believer and the reason why they have proliferated even in nations where constitutional liberty would seem to have rendered them otiose is that in just the same countries many formerly reliable devices of identification (such as class, or region, or religion) have become less reliable. Beliefs supply a ready and easy way of creating immediate relationships – of both alliance and hostility – between people; they are co-ordinates, as it were, of the personality. They are platforms for people to stand on. In discovering how we react to general beliefs, we may often discover otherwise less accessible developments within the personality. Our awareness of this matter is further complicated by the fact that we generally wish not merely to identify ourselves, but to identify ourselves as superior, and we are capable of going to quite extraordinary lengths in order to do so.

Society may, then, be regarded as a field not only of people but also of beliefs, and general beliefs, especially where they touch upon religion and politics, are much the most dominant. Academic inquiry is a sub-class of beliefs which must somehow sustain a separate identity against the constant and often insidious pressure of these general beliefs. Furthermore, general beliefs are not random atoms but are subject to clustering. Consider for example that line of thought, with antecedents centuries old, which finds in society a natural ordering; which takes great pride in the achievements and triumphs of one's country; which pays a respectful attention to the doings and commands of those set in authority over us; and which has a dislike of radical politics. It can only be imperfectly specified because although it might be given a name (such as Toryism) and although there are plenty of people who share most of it, there are many others who accept one part and not another. George Orwell is a celebrated example. Further, it is a line of thought which cannot convincingly be located in any particular area of society: it is found among dukes, and among gravediggers. Some profligates hold it, and so do some prigs. In spite of this indeterminacy, it is very commonly (but not invariably) associated with what we may call a supportive rhetoric, and it is this supportive rhetoric which gives us the clue to some of its identificatory functions. It presents people holding this cluster of general beliefs as being honest, respectable, hardworking and honourable. One holder of this cluster of beliefs is likely to accord such moral characteristics to another holder. Sometimes, further, the holding of these opinions is taken as a licence to regard with contempt the shiftless, the spendthrifts and the discontented of the world. Exactly how honourable and virtuous such people are, of course, is a highly variable matter: in *all* the cases we are considering, opinion is a poor guide to value.

Consider, alternatively, that philosophy (in the popular sense of the term) which is republican or socialist in politics, utilitarian in morals, agnostic or atheist in religion, and progressive in its view of social development. Like any other cluster of beliefs, this one may be found at the level of clubhouse chat, or of quite elaborate intellectuality. This tradition too has its supportive rhetoric: it presents itself as the set of conclusions arrived at by people who are questioning and critical and have the capacity to 'think for themselves', while its opponents are often characterized as snobbish, conformist, pious, prejudiced, superstitious, and victimized by wishful thinking.

In these terms, society is constituted of loose alliances of belief. Certainly, there is no logic to the matter. For if the two clusters we have mentioned are called Tory and Progressive, there is no item of the Tory creed which cannot (and has not often) been held by those who are predominantly Progressive; and the converse also holds true. It is indeed the case that in the course of actual discussion, appeals to consistency may be made; and there will be attempts to show that a Progressive cannot consistently believe that a woman's place is in the home (which will be stigmatized as derived from a Tory notion of natural ordering); or that a Tory ought consistently to hold religious beliefs of a theistic kind. But these sallies are merely diversionary tactics in the endless battle of beliefs of which society is constituted. Each belief, for all the apparent clustering, is adventuring for support on its own. And just as there is no logical connection between these general beliefs, so also there is no sociological connection. They may be found among any class of person at all. It is not true that a fervent belief in property is held only or primarily by owners of property – often, indeed, the contrary; nor is it true that 'male chauvinists' are the only ones to believe that a woman's place is in the home; and so on. And a final general comment on this battle of beliefs may be made: that just as the real point of a good deal of general believing is self-identification, so general beliefs are closely involved with vanity. It is rare to find a person asserting this kind of practical attitude without also at the same time flattering himself as possessing some admirable moral quality.

One of the dangers to academic inquiry consequent upon this social situation may be found in the fact that the Progressive tradition often chooses to identify itself in a manner close to various kinds of academic self-characterization: as being critical, questioning, and resistant to current orthodoxies. The rhetorical function of this form of self-identification is to strengthen Progressive beliefs by drawing upon academic prestige. It is entirely normal and legitimate that this attempt should be made; but it is equally necessary that universities should resist any attempt to involve themselves in a battle of beliefs to which their own concerns are essentially tangential. They lose their academic identity whenever they sink themselves in a social or political cause, even one which (like many Progressive causes) presents itself in apparently congenial terms.

To contemplate general beliefs in terms of truth and error would be to fall into a version of the monism we discussed in the last section. For as with many things in the practical world, this swarming of general beliefs can only be understood backwards. It looks superficially as if we first arrive at a general conclusion and then approve or disapprove because of it. But our approvals and disapprovals are often immediate and spontaneous emotions, adept at defensive rationalization. It would seem plausible to think that our

111

approvals determine our general beliefs, rather than the converse. And if this is so, then we may understand why so much of our spare time is spent in contemplating the general beliefs of others: to service our general beliefs by the constant cultivation of approval and disapproval towards those of others is to keep one of the major instruments of the passions in good working order. Should anyone doubt this intimate involvement between general beliefs and the passions, he has only to remember that the mental life of the general believer (and there can be very few educated people these days who are not at some level of seriousness to be counted such) is a ceaseless movement between the pleasure which comes when the world appears to confirm his beliefs, and the pain and gloom (often followed by hasty rationalization) which comes on those occasions when the world is admitted not to accord with his expectations. The follower of Woman's Liberation finds pleasure in reports about the miseries of housebound women, while the believer in a traditional role for women seizes upon higher divorce rates and goes on to diagnose lack of fulfilment in the career girl. An Afrikaner nationalist takes pleasure in political disorders in Black Africa, for he knew it would happen all along, and is correspondingly displeased by instances of African political or technical competence. A communist takes pleasure in the achievements of the Soviet Union, and finds many things about the Stalinist purges of the thirties a bitter pill to swallow. Indeed, for several decades many communists actually succeeded in not swallowing this particular pill at all. For the really dedicated general believer always has the option of dismissing what he finds unpleasant as lies, exaggerations or failures to see things in perspective.

What needs to be noticed about both the pleasures and the pains of general believing is that they rest upon a practical sense of consistency having no relation to academic standards. For an academic would consider that, in the Russian case just mentioned, neither failure nor success tells us anything very conclusive about the ideological system of communism. Russia is one thing, communism another; both are immensely complicated, and if we have to judge whether success or failure (which are already heavily generalized conclusions of reasoning and statistics) are to be attributed to the one or the other, then we simply do not have the evidence to do it. An academic inquiry takes place in terms of hypothetical reasoning, while the test of general beliefs in the practical world depends upon quite different forensic or debating rules. The measure of a general believer's embarrassment is a claim he has previously made; and since a communist (to continue this example) has announced his belief that communism will be the salvation of Russia, so he must accept whatever consequences are evidently damnable. A similar type of embarrassment is the price any general believer is likely to have to make for his commitment. In the quarrelsome jostling of general beliefs, there are conventions of consistency to be observed by which the same kind of fact which will please a believer in some circumstances must be allowed to embarrass him in another.

Society is an intellectual battleground of general beliefs. And among educated people a great deal of knowledge and ingenuity will be available to buttress such general beliefs. In this area, the danger to universities comes not from the fact that they will be held in low esteem, but rather that they become the final court of appeal for general believers. For it has long been the case that universities have thrown off a stream of reports, experiments, hypotheses and judgements which may be taken as supporting or weakening one or other common general belief. It will be clear that, in terms of the argument of this book, such supporting or weakening is based upon a misunderstanding of the hypothetical character of the academic. But this misunderstanding has not prevented the mounting of many strong pressures upon the universities to support 'open-minded', 'unprejudiced', 'disinterested' or 'objectively valid' general beliefs. In other words, general beliefs which characterize themselves as virtuous press upon the universities for a support which the

113

universities cannot give because their sole allegiance is to truth, and further, to a truth conceived differently from the way it is found in the world. Such is the general situation with which we now have to deal.

We shall find that the area in which general beliefs are most prone to appear indistinguishable from academic inquiry are, first, intellectual journalism, which is generally the first and sometimes the only contact many educated people have with the academic world; and secondly ideology, which is the conversion of religious or political demands into an academic idiom. The resulting confusions require that we should deal with each of these in turn. But it is possible to sum up the general position very simply: all academic inquiry is intellectual, but a great deal of intellectuality is not academic. Most mistakes about universities derive from confusing the one thing with the other.

6 Journalism: Nutshell Truths for the Breakfast Table

The world of journalism, especially intellectual journalism, has close affinities with the academic world: so close that, unless we look carefully, we shall miss the difference. Journalism arises from a generalized curiosity remote from practical concerns. The man who takes in the latest *coup d'état* and the newest argument about life on other planets along with his breakfast orange juice is not doing anything relevant to his workaday concerns. And a good deal of journalism, especially in what is commonly called the 'quality press', is not only concerned with academic subjects, but is actually written by academics themselves. Hence our argument thus far, distinguishing between the practical and the academic worlds, would seem to licence the conclusion that nothing very fundamental separates serious journalism from academic argument. Yet, while it may be freely admitted that such periodicals as the *New York Review of Books*, the *Times Literary Supplement* and *Encounter* often contain borderline cases, nonetheless journalism and the university must be taken as two quite separate worlds which are all the more dangerous to each other's identity by virtue of their evident kinship.

It is clear that if we take journalism to be a 'world' of its own, with an organized and distinguishable view of reality, then we shall not be concerned merely with newspapers and magazines. We shall certainly have to include radio and television and everything else that is covered by the term 'mass media'. And we shall also have to take in the vast number of books and articles intended for the general reader, without which publishing would virtually collapse: the vast field of 'popularization' whose categories are the same as those of journalism. But such a category of journalism cannot even stop here: it must expand to take in most artistic products which can be classed as 'entertainment' rather than art. And it must also include many textbooks intended for students. We are dealing, then, with intellectually perishable commodities, and this fact alone allows us immediately to make one central point: that it is both the triumph and the disaster of journalism to be so exactly attuned to the moment of its production that any single example of it looks odd if it should be viewed at a later time. It follows from this, of course, that journalism is an excellent clue for any historian who seeks the atmosphere of a lost epoch.

Journalism is primarily a commerce in information, and the strength of the modern newspaper is that it performs a great variety of functions which were not hitherto united. Modern journalism derives, in part, from the letters exchanged in times past by the leisured classes of Europe. These letters sometimes slaked a general curiosity about well-known personalities or foreign customs; and sometimes, particularly in the case of kings and ministers, they constituted a form of intelligence and advice about affairs of state. This epistolary ancestry survives in the journalistic terminology of 'correspondents' and 'letters from abroad'. Another remote source of journalism is in the almost instinctive human disposition to chronicle significant events – a task undertaken in Europe at one time by monks, who used the margins of their Easter calculations to record what they thought was significant. But between these monks and a modern newspaperman there is a huge gulf which may, in part, be measured by the fact that a newspaperman will

116

always find news, whereas it was not unusual for the monks to dismiss an entire year with the words: 'Nothing memorable happened.' Among later attempts to rescue memorable events from the tides of time were the eighteenth-century *Annual Register* and the *Daily Universal Register* of 1785, from which *The Times* is directly descended.

These impulses towards the creation of newspapers came in time to be supplemented by political developments. The modern state has involved itself more and more continuously in the daily lives of its subjects, and has long needed ways of communicating its decisions to the population at large. The distribution of written proclamations, announcements in local assemblies and the services of the local town crier could, with the growth of literacy, be supplemented by newspapers and gazettes. Furthermore, it came to be useful, if also at times painful, for a government to know what its subjects were thinking. Ever since the invention of printing each large European political crisis produced a flow of pamphlets of opinion; by the seventeenth century this flow was sufficiently continuous to be accommodated within a regular format. The social circumstances facilitating this are obvious enough: the concentration of people in cities, and the mechanical facility of the printing presses. Like much else, newspapers are commonly attributed to the set of people known in the textbook as the 'middle classes': a set of people who, according to these same textbooks, have never ceased to increase. It was certainly true that a very large gap had opened up between the illiterate farmer's labourer, whose world was largely circumscribed by his village, and the urban sophisticate whose head was buzzing with the unfolding story of politics and of arts and letters.

The emergence of the newspaper from this varied collection of separate endeavours typifies the strength and weakness of the modern world. The modern newspaper, compared with its more specialized predecessors, is enormously fast, efficient and resourceful. No medieval prince had at his elbow so reliable and professional a source of information and appraisal as is available to the intelligent modern newspaper reader. The information may not be entirely reliable, but when was such information ever so? What it lacks in reliability it makes up for in abundance, particularly abundance of sources of information which may be checked off against each other. But because information in earlier times was directed towards a specific person, it could explore subtleties and indulge in nuances which are impossible for a modern journalist addressing a generalized reader. In place of the letter-writer's knowledge of his correspondent's interest and temperament has come a generalized substitute: the concept of 'news'.

For we have noted that journalism is a commerce in information. But as the consumer of the information becomes a vague figure, it becomes more and more difficult to select from infinite availability the information he might want to read. Utility is, for some purposes, a good enough test, but the makers of newspapers needed to go beyond it. What readers seek is sensations. And the criterion of the information and the ideas to be presented in a newspaper becomes whatever will excite indignation, elation, horror, amusement, pity, complacency, and the rest of the human repertoire of emotions about public events. The rules are clear and evident enough: near events are news in a way that distant ones are not; one hundred dead is a larger news story than ten dead; events involving well-known personalities are news in a way that events involving unknown people are not; and any event that an ordinary man would begin telling with such words as 'you won't believe this, but . . .' will make good copy. There are plenty of rules, and some stories write themselves; but, as any apprentice journalist is constantly told, it takes a form of intuition to recognize a good news story, and it is the quality of this intuition which makes a great journalist. An outsider is likely to be sceptical of such intuitions. They accord to the concept of news a bogus objectivity. For 'news' is, to a large extent, whatever journalists think it is. And so long as they do not bore us they will transmit to us whatever judgements they make themselves.

But whatever actually does count as news, nothing is news for very long. There are indeed crises which dominate the front page for weeks on end, but only by supplying a succession of new events or pseudo-events. The greatest of stories must come to an end, but it will gain a certain immortality in being frequently revived in later features and programmes of nostalgia. What this makes clear is that journalism is primarily a form of distraction and entertainment. The only really fundamental fault is to lose the audience from boredom. A newspaper is no place for the man with a ruling obsession, and the one certainty of journalism, as of ladies' fashions, is the inevitability of change. The whirligig of fashion determines all journalism, including the most solemn and portentous. In the 1950s, for example, it was a general fashion to favour stories relating to the gap between the economies of rich and poor states. This preoccupation had succeeded an earlier sensitivity to the dangers of an all-out nuclear war, and was, in its turn, superseded by the emergence of a new (and no doubt, in time, equally disposable) interest in the environmental pollution caused by modern industry. Such fashions as this are directly relevant to our theme, because there is no doubt that they play a large part in determining both the availability of money for academic research and the disposition of researchers to work on some problems rather than others. This is but one of the many points at which worldly preoccupations, as articulated in journalism, exert a powerful and generally capricious effect upon the internal coherence of the academic world.

We have so far taken it for granted that a news story is something so luminous as to be recognized by inspection: something which, to use the most natural word, 'just happens'. It is certainly the case that both the writers and the readers of newspapers have no difficulty in recognizing a murder, an airline disaster, or the national budget as being, quite inevitably, 'news'. But the case of those early medieval monks who might write 'nothing memorable happened' about a twelve-month stretch of time cautions us that the matter is more complex than might appear. Were the monks simply like unimaginative letter-writers for whom 'nothing much seems to have happened'? And what is the talent of the good letter-writer who can conjure events out of an apparently featureless drabness of time? The answer is that the good letter-writer 'builds up' the events by pointing to features of reality in terms of which quite small things take on the impact of news. And this is exactly what a journalist must do in constructing a newspaper: his product depends upon the extensive use of 'background'. A *coup d'état* in a small African or Central American republic, or a new economic statistic, are events which only become news if they are set like jewels within a large and extensive context of background and interpretation. The more one looks at a news story, particularly a continuing one such as an international crisis, the more it becomes clear that this element of 'background' is not only vital to its construction but that it also takes up very much more space than the actual event itself.

It will also be clear that the 'quality press' is to be distinguished from the 'popular press' largely by the quantity and type of background used. It needs a great deal of background to discover news in an international crisis, but very little to establish a brutal murder or a sexual scandal. Of course, there always *is* background to be added: and a murder or a sex scandal, which are most obviously stories for the popular press, may be transformed into stories for the quality press by the addition of sociological or literary background. The archetype of this kind of transfer is the case where quality newspapers hire celebrated intellectuals to cover spectacular trials. All newspapers necessarily build up a constant pressure of background: in the popular press, this is often to be found in identificatory material about personalities – material which is necessary in order to guarantee a constant flow of almost automatic news about ordinary events in the lives of people rendered extraordinary by the attention which has been paid to their background. Quality papers, while using all the same techniques, specialize in political news which is virtually incomprehensible without a great deal of background in the mind of the reader.

The importance of background is clearly recognized by working journalists themselves: 'Instantaneous, raw and in bulk news is an indigestible commodity. It needs processing. The editorial processes of newspapers provide insight and perspective to public happenings; they enable them to be presented in terms that fall within the experience and judge-ment of readers . . .'[1] An event and its interpretation: such is the familiar way in which journalists understand their own activity. Yet anyone of philosophical inclinations will find himself suspicious at seeing an activity explained in terms of a given set of materials and what is done with them; of the raw indigestible facts contrasted with their cooking; of data sustaining theory. For, given that one possible response to the world is in terms of 'nothing memorable happened', it is necessary to consider the possibility that events are not observed and interpreted, but rather that they are them-selves constructions. Interpretation begins, in other words, not merely with the 'background' but with the actual event itself. For the events are specified by such names as 'depres-sion', 'revolution', 'scandal', 'gun battle', 'environmental pollution', 'airline tragedy', and so on, and all such terms – indeed, *all* terms used to describe events – are themselves already theories about what in reality has actually happened.

The argument I am presenting is one which will be familiar to sophisticated readers, and has appeared in a variety of places: in the literary theory of the *nouveau roman*, in the phenomenological analysis of experience, in Marxist social theory, and in some analysis of the logic of historical explanation. In each case, the argument appears in a different form; in all cases, it depends upon the age-old

[1] Francis Williams, *The Right to Know*, London 1969, p. 3.

philosophical device which will never allow of the existence of materials of the understanding to which the understanding itself has contributed nothing. And within journalism the currency of this argument has had the curious effect of undermining one of the earlier and most respected of journalistic shibboleths : that fact is sacred while comment is free. For, some journalists have argued, if even the event itself reflects the mind of the reporter, why strive to keep a story free from political comment? Or, to put the matter another way, one implication drawn from this analysis is that there is no fundamental difference between journalism and propaganda – an implication which has led the self-righteous to believe that journalism should become *their* propaganda. In the course of the 1960s, reporters began to turn their news stories into pseudo-profound commentaries. The implication, however, is false. For while it is true that all events are constructed, they are not all constructed in the same way. And journalism itself can, I think, be shown to have its own distinctive mode of event construction which marks it off very clearly indeed from propaganda.

Our argument is, then, that journalism does not simply reflect the common man's instinctive interest in change and novelty, but that in part it creates this interest and determines its direction. Journalism is not simply one social activity among others, but is a pervasive modern manner of understanding reality : it is, in fact, the world construed as a succession of novelties, and it breeds impatience with the static, the repetitive, the mechanical or anything else which is seen as a mere process. For this reason, the common journalistic cliché that 'we live in a changing world', along with the many prescriptions about how important it is to make appropriate responses to this change, must be seen not as (what it sometimes seems) a piece of hysteria, but rather as the operative assumption of the journalistic view of reality. All readers of newspapers, which is to say virtually all of us, share this view of reality. And in specifying journalism in this way, we have immediately distinguished it from propaganda: for propaganda is the treatment of events not as novelties but as confirmations of a doctrine already held. Further, the general beliefs confirmed are already built into the terms out of which the events are constructed. These beliefs are revealed in such terms as 'progressive' or 'reactionary', 'colonialist' or 'privileged'.

The journalistic view of reality is so widespread and pervasive that it has generated its own theory of education: namely, that the business of education is to provide the knowledge necessary to understand the world we live in – i.e., the knowledge necessary to read the newspapers. History, geography, science and mathematics are journalistically approved as performing this function in a way in which the classical studies do not, and there has been a strong and continuous pressure to introduce into schools such pre-eminently 'background' studies as politics, economics and sociology. These questions may, of course, be studied academically; in terms of the earlier distinction we have used between grammar books and phrase books, each of these subjects may be studied as 'grammars'. But what is journalistically demanded is a 'phrase book' in which we study the politics of (say) Red China, not because of any academic significance it may have, nor because anything very much is known about it (for it is, politically speaking, a dark continent), but because it often gets into the headlines. Here is a conception of education entirely determined by a limited conception of something called (for purposes of persuasion) 'the modern world', a conception which acts as a screen determining what shall be admitted or rejected. The effect of such a criterion of what should be taught is to render education rigid and static; which is to say, to destroy it as education altogether. And this fact is itself recognized by its own promoters in their fears that what is taught in schools and universities soon becomes 'out of date' and needs to be replaced. The replacement will, of course, be supplied merely by a new set of required 'phrases'. Here we meet for the first but not the last time the paradox that an overwhelmingly explicit concern with responding to change causes a permanent (and slightly hysterical) immobility.

The belief that the function of education is to prepare the mind of man for the experience of reading the quality press has a converse: that reading these newspapers is a part of education. Certainly it is the case that in many subjects pupils are encouraged to read the higher journalism and to regard such reading as a virtuous and profitable activity. And the reason for this is, in part, a tendency in quality newspapers to concern themselves less with what is actually happening than with forms of background that bear a superficial resemblance to many subjects studied at school. The very model of this tendency towards the predominance of background is the obituary, in which the event eliciting the story is a mere physiological process, and the entire story consists of the background. The case is the same with the extensive use of anniversaries, as we shall see when we consider intellectual journalism. And everywhere in journalism is to be found the feature article which is loosely tied to the events of the world.

We have noted that what is popularly called 'quality' in a newspaper consists of large quantities of background, particularly political and economic background: the background without which no event may be saved from the flux of trivialities arising merely from the processes of human life. This material reaches its perfection in weekly or monthly journals of opinion in which the events become simply the starting point for background and speculation in terms of what is developing and what is likely to happen. It is in this area that we may first begin to notice the element of self-congratulation in journalism: it becomes a vehicle of *knowledgeability*. Journalistic sophistication is a loose and confident grip on the meaning of things. It takes over from academic studies some of the accoutrements of historical profundity, and begins to talk of eras, seminal contribution, epochs, archetypal events, and similar things. Paradoxically, this apparently more sophisticated writing is a good deal easier to turn out than old-fashioned 'hard news', and quality journalism is subject to a kind of intellectual pleurisy in which totally automatic bits of profundity are passed off as intelligent appreciations of the course of events. When, for example, the educational correspondent of *The Times* writes: 'For better or worse, the riot at the Garden House hotel was a turning point in the history of university discipline at Cambridge, and by extension at Oxford too. Whatever the committee decides, the proctorial system can never be quite the same again',[2] we may recognize the journalistic equivalent of the placebo or the bromide, effortless, empty, forgettable, but supplying the easy surrogate of historical profundity which journalism encourages us to expect.

But long before journalism shows signs of being afflicted with this fatal *folie de grandeur*, two odd things have become evident. The first is that journalistic profundity involves being able to guess the future course of events in order to assess the significance of what is happening now. The journalist, as we shall see, vainly attempts to cheat the historian of his business by working out at the time what is significant and what is to be ignored in the present world. This attempt is, of course, logically impossible, since these attempts to guess the future are themselves a part of the present and can never escape from it. But in the pursuit of this objective, journalists are to be found devoting more and more time and attention not to reporting present events, but to trying to guess future ones. Thus the really significant feature of background, which we have not yet considered, is that a good deal of it consists of guesses as to the way things are going, and virtually all reporting of events is affected by that endeavour. This is why newspapers are so preoccupied with terms like 'promise' and 'prospects' and 'likely moves' and the rest of the futuristic vocabulary. A kind of febrile eagerness to know the future begins to haunt the journalist and, to some extent, his audience. During the 1970 General Election in Britain, the BBC was able to fill up

[2] 25 October 1970.

some of its time by reporting its prediction, made about an hour or so before the actual results appeared, of how one constituency would vote. The relative accuracy of this prediction (based upon asking people emerging from polling booths how they had, in fact, voted) was counted a great triumph. That anything, any guess or straw in the wind, no matter how vacuous, is better than a quiet mind, seems to be the assumption on which this and other similar exercises in divination are based. And although part of this disposition may be attributed to the vast quantities of newspaper space and broadcasting time that must be filled, an even larger part must be attributed to our having learned a close and continuous involvement, by virtue of journalism, with our collective hopes and fears.

The second thing which becomes evident is that, paradoxically, journalism as the pursuit of news and novelty ends by presenting to us a fundamentally changeless world. This fact is most easily seen in the case of the popular press, where a diet of abandoned brides, errant clergymen, adventures of pets, aircraft accidents, bizarre and touching coincidences, wars and earthquakes has but the most tenuous of relations to any reality. It is true that the abandoned brides and their newsworthy companions have ascertainable names and circumstances; but any competent journalist could easily invent them, and public relations experts sometimes do so. That this is not so evident in the quality press is only because of the apparent solidity of the background, but here too the careers of popes, prime ministers and demagogues pursuing their switchback career through the ups and downs of journalistic fashion have a perceptible sameness to the ordinary intelligent reader, the one whose education tempts him to mumble *plus ça change* as he approaches the dense columns of his favourite heavy. Besides, the news must often seem a superficial thing compared to the deep organic rhythms of the advice on Christmas present-buying, the regular features on how to bring up children or keep husbands happy, and the summer-holiday supplements which begin to appear immediately after Christmas.

But, unless we are dealing with bad journalism, the reflection that the newspapers exhibit what Charles Dickens once called the 'monotony of perpetual change' would only arise in rare moods. For it is the considerable virtue of journalism to convert the world into a diverting and amusing spectacle. The diversion includes, of course, many a thrill of horror at the thought of over-population and the imminence of Armageddon, but diverting it fundamentally is. And if journalism is to have such virtue, then it must accept the limitations which any virtue involves. An editor must always be able to gauge the moment when a news story has worn out its welcome, the moment when it must sink to a few lowly paragraphs on an inside page. It is not his business to keep the sufferings of a suffering humanity in a proper focus. And just as a journalist must not feel too much (conventional expressions of indignation and pity will suffice), so too he must not know too much. Detail and nuance, indeed any kind of real complexity, are fatal to the smooth contours of a good story. Journalism is a skilled profession requiring detachment and a certain kind of insensitivity to the truth of things – though never an insensitivity to (what is sometimes confused with the truth of things) the facts: the age of a film star, the address of a victim, or the precise number of clauses in a treaty.

Journalism is, as I have characterized it, a superficial activity, its seriousness mere solemnity, even its indignation merely a carnival mask of the trade. It rides the surface of things. It is a certain manner of viewing reality and it must be analysed in any discussion of education because, as we have seen, its articulation has created, among many auxiliary pieces of equipment, something we may call the journalistic theory of education. But journalism affects education not only by this statement of its demands in the form of an educational theory, but also by the demands which people addicted to journalism will make upon schools and universities. They will demand 'relevance', and complain of scholasticism if what they are taught in schools fails to supply them with the same kind of relevance which they find in newspapers. The relation of journalism to our theme is even closer than this would suggest, for journalism, as a manner of understanding reality, has naturally moved on to the understanding of academic reality, subsuming the events of the academic world within its own categories.

The publication of a book or the elaboration of a theory is, to an educated public, 'news'. Such events have their own complicated academic context and may be adequately understood only by the small public familiar with the past from which they emerge. But for journalism, such events must be exhibited as part of the general world of novelties which can be made accessible to the newspaper's public. There are, of course, very varying levels of sophistication at which this may be done: at the most primitive level, science becomes news by a simple conversion into magic and power: it has to do with wonder drugs and rockets, and is in general misleadingly understood as that which supplies the knowledge for industrial technology. In slightly more elevated terms, the promulgation of a new scientific theory becomes one more item to be added to a set of 'discoveries' which appear to constitute a body of knowledge often called 'scientific truth'. It is at this level of sophistication that intellectual issues can become public questions, as most notably in the debates about the consonance of 'science' and 'religion' which were particularly fashionable in the nineteenth century. But even at this level, it is common for scientific theories to be seen as essentially the outcome of personal strivings and laboratory endeavours. The scientist appears at this level in entertainment fiction, or historical legends which describe the triumph of heroic rebels against encrusted tradition. Similarly, if a new book on any other kind of academic subject is to become the subject matter for journalism, then it must be ransacked for startling revelations, a comprehensible thesis, or at least some point of contact with the experience of the readers. It must, to put the matter at its most brutal, cease to be an academic work at all, and must be treated as if it were a work of popularization.

This kind of transformation will be found at any level of intellectual journalism. Thus, to take an example at random, *The Times* publishes an excellent series of reports of experiments first recorded in scientific technical journals, and it converts them to journalistic use by making a connection with the experience of its readers. Thus very elaborate explorations of fossilized ice, bearing upon theories of climatic change, are presented under the headline: 'It Will Be Colder In 1995'.[3] Science tends always to appear as a technological process, and hypotheses take on the hard certainty of 'discoveries'. If a direct academic contrast to this journalistic attitude be required, nothing better can be found than a disdainful remark made at the end of a public lecture by the philosopher J. D. Austin: 'It is not unusual for an audience at a lecture to include some who prefer things to be important, and to them now, in case there are any such present, there is owed a peroration. Why, in short, does all this matter?'[4]

Intellectual journalism, then, to the extent that it deals with the academic world, must assimilate what it takes to some kind of formula. The formula specifies what is necessary to make good journalism. One term of this formula is a consideration of space available; another covers what kind of showing any particular item may make in the daily or weekly constellation of news. Other terms of the formula include the assimilation of strange material to the comprehensibility of the readers. Still other terms of the formula relate to the mechanisms of a journalistic story, whereby the most striking point of the story must become the 'intro', which is then followed by related items linked together so as to draw the

[3] 23 October 1969.
[4] 'Ifs and Cans', in *Studies in Philosophy: British Academy Lectures*, Oxford 1956, p. 140.

reader on. In many cases of intellectual journalism this introduction is likely to be some academically remote popular preoccupation. And the fact that journalism is the world organized as a succession of novelties applies to intellectual journalism in the same way as it applies to the treatment of events: once a book, or a theory, has been a news item for some time, it must be superseded by other quite unrelated items, lest the reader should become bored. There are, of course, intellectual periodicals where the pressure of the formula applies with less rigour than that described here; but in journalism, the formula is always present: the line is always being cast towards the largest concentration of an interested public.

And, it is necessary to add, why not? For it needs to be emphasized that the world legitimately contains both journalism (as one branch of the practical commerce with ideas) and also academic inquiry. Each is defective in terms of the other. From a journalist's point of view, academic life is full of fiddling and pedantic concerns. The courageous embrace of minutiae looks like the occupational vice of the academic profession. An academic, on the other hand, is likely to regard journalism as being slick and superficial, concerned only with the sensational, and determined to discover a fixity and a certainty in academic conclusions which no academic believes them to have. We have already noted the human propensity towards self-identification as superior to a neighbour. It applies here. Just as the academic may regard the journalist as a brash parasite, so intellectual journalists tend to regard themselves as sensible men poised between the trivialities of the popular press and the pedantries of the academic. But we need not take too seriously these skirmishes in the moral life of human beings, for there is no external criterion in terms of which the dispute might be adjudicated. But great confusion follows from failure to recognize the clear distinction between the journalistic and the academic views of the world – even though such a recognition does not entail that any actual piece of writing may be homogeneously assigned to one category or another. Most can, but some cannot.

Journalism does indeed distort whatever it touches, but its distortions are often illuminating and they are generally unavoidable. For in a large and complex world, we have no alternative but to apprehend things by means of the image and the stereotype. Among unsophisticated people, images and stereotypes are commonly taken to be real things, objects for veneration or for hatred. Journalism must needs turn the world into a huge parish, supplying us with fake intimacies and the illusion of direct comprehension. Because the world is big, we must recognize its inhabitants and their opinions by the crudest of signs.

In intellectual matters, identifications must be made in terms of conventional values: Lawrence, Russell, Wittgenstein, Einstein, Teilhard de Chardin – not to mention the ubiquitous mandarins of intellectual journalism, Freud and Marx – are cultural tokens with which the intellectual journalist may nudge the mind of his audience. What is said about these tags is likely to amount to a cliché, and then to become the subject not of critical discussion, but of a kind of intellectual knockabout: clichés can be inverted and transposed and recombined to yield paradoxes or daring utterances, and if the ingenuity is sufficient, many highly entertaining and sometimes illuminating things may be said. To those for whom the subject matter is more than a collection of tokens, intellectual journalism may well provide one kind of extramural stimulus that helps to fuel academic work. But much more commonly this unnatural vivacity of clichés must be taken simply as an entertainment which week after week will tickle the understanding but leave it in the same condition as before.

For journalism is necessarily trapped in its own world. Condemned to dealing with the surface of things, it tries to defeat this limitation by the promise of exposure, of the inside story, and of taking the reader 'behind the scenes'. But the 'inside' story turns out to be another version of the public

131

face, and the supposedly intimate revelations as much the subject of careful calculation as the recently abandoned surface. It is the same with the vivacity of intellectual journalism. Academic work consists in a slow revolving of questions and answers in which the new questions are generated directly by the defects of the previous answers. The principle of change is organic, and the fact that new developments build upon a long tradition of similar work is signalled in footnotes. The academic world has a long memory. Journalism, by contrast, has virtually no memory at all. A book reviewer takes off from the intellectual equipment of his audience, and once he has spoken he will not constitute the starting point for later work. In journalism, the principle of change is mechanical in the sense that what is written responds to the outside pressure of pleasing an audience. It is a capricious and, to some extent, unpredictable audience. Since journalism is about novelty, a story that fatigues an audience must be replaced by another story which does not. Each week there is an issue to be filled, and the content must vary only within the constant formula. The journalist picks over the events of his world – anniversaries, recently published books, scientific congresses, news items with an associated intellectual content – and seeks those which can be converted into news. The cult of anniversaries in the intellectual press is the quintessence of journalism: it supplies a totally random and mechanical reason for taking an interest in some man or event.

The mechanical character of journalism is a direct consequence of what one may call, with only slight exaggeration, its logic. For the classical question, 'what's new?' – the searchlight the experienced journalist turns upon reality – bends the answer in a particular direction. A popular journalist will always find something of human interest in any situation – for nothing else really excites his readers. A more intellectual journalist, however, will find something not very much less circumscribed: he will find that an old guard is being overthrown, a crisis is taking place, a power struggle is in progress, a generation gap is being exemplified, or a revolution has occurred. These general ideas may be treated, at will, as either the clichés of the journalistic trade, or the logically organizing ideas of the journalist view of reality. Crisis, Revolution, Gap, etc exemplify the kinds of ideas which determine what is visible to the journalistic eye. There is, of course, always more going on than what is visible in this manner, but only a historian or a novelist or, perhaps, someone who has given his life (rather than a few days of his professional attention) to the situation will begin to know what it is. Journalists and their readers seek not understanding, but a rather different kind of grip on reality which we might suitably call 'knowledgeability'; and understanding is positively inimical to knowledgeability. This point is brilliantly made in a throwaway line written by a journalist reflecting on the dispositions appropriate to his profession: helpful qualities in a journalist include 'a reluctance to understand too much too well (because *tout comprendre c'est tout pardonner* and *tout pardonner* makes dull copy)'.[5]

Journalism is thus not only the world presented as a succession of novelties, it also highlights the persons who become news in melodramatic terms: as the bearers of triumph, disaster, crisis, failure or brilliance. It is to the understanding what melodrama is to art; the ellipsis by which a historian makes a statement like 'Napoleon won the battle of Austerlitz' becomes in journalism a consistent distortion of the world – a distortion commonly found so pleasurable by the consumers of journalism that they will go to enormous lengths to become subject to it. Herostratus, a man of no otherwise visible talent who burned down the temple at Delphi in order to immortalize his name, has many imitators among the many for whom newspapers are the only annals of immortality available.

When it comes to treating intellectual matters, then, journalism inevitably brings in its train a degree of excess. It has a Great Ideas and Great Men notion of culture. It can

[5] Nicholas Tomalin in the *Sunday Times*, 26 October 1969.

recognize its objects only by single attitudes or combinations of attitudes; but it is not too far from the truth to say that it tends to oscillate between adulation and debunking, and that these two attitudes, apparently contradictory, are two sides of the same kind of preoccupation. Children have a tendency to ignore the dough and concentrate on the currants in the pudding; and thus before long to induce nausea in themselves. The world of journalism is not greatly different. Just as in political matters, journalists must produce objectivity by operating with the mechanical criterion of 'showing both sides of the question', so also in intellectual matters they are the victims of contrasting and contradictory extremes, corresponding to the two most primitive attitudes we may have to the world, those of approval and disapproval. It is, however, only the visible highlights of the world which are eligible for this kind of ingenious mechanical attitude to the world. Newsworthy intellectuals are severed from their context, become prophets or 'modern masters', and teeter on the edge of absurdity, for their real element is the fluid medium of academic or artistic controversy.

Journalism as we have discussed it is a criterion for organizing knowledge and information, and however intellectual it may be, it has a significantly different organization and content from that of the academic world. The same thing is commonly true of textbooks, which live in a shadowy region somewhere between the academic and the practical worlds. The significant thing about a textbook is that it is tailored to the presumed limitations of its readers. In schools, some concern for the character of the audience is unavoidable, but in universities it has much less place, for the essence of a university education is that it consists less in the direct provision of knowledge than in a juxtaposition of the scholarly and those who actively seek to learn. The place of undergraduates in a university is, on our argument, to be allowed to listen to people who are not exclusively concerned with the business of teaching the young. The proper materials for the use of undergraduates, therefore, consist not of textbooks, but of texts, which are actual writings within a particular discipline, generally intended for other sophisticated people, and which are also thought to exhibit a masterly grip upon the logic and kind of sophistication which the inquiry involves. Where education is based on texts, the undergraduate has the responsibility of submitting his understanding to subjects he studies. It is barely an exaggeration to say that the textbook is constructed upon the opposite principle. For one thing, it writes down to its audience. For another, all but exceptional textbooks operate with the essentially journalistic criterion of mainstream and tributary: for textbooks generally purport to be explaining to their readers what is simple and basic in their subjects, as a preliminary to embarking upon the problem-infested areas located at what the textbooks encourage us to think of as the frontiers of knowledge. The tendency of most textbooks is, therefore, to encourage a simple and unphilosophical reception of the current categorization of a subject. Most textbooks go out of date rapidly, and this is a further measure of the extent to which they are concerned with 'phrases' rather than with 'grammars'.

Intellectual journalism crossed with the textbook generates popularization, which is a slice of the academic world detached from the process of discussion in which it is embedded. It is attractive by virtue of its combination of entertainment with improvement. The element of entertainment is essential, because the reader of a work of popularization is assumed not to have a strong and serious interest in the subject. Such a reader must be lured into reading the book by a constant exhibition of the connection between the subject of the book and the ordinary life of the reader; certainly he must be spared any dry technicalities. An academic who, in his own world, is an inquirer, appears primarily in this part of the practical world in the guise of an expert. Sometimes (and commonly in self-defence) the popularizer adopts the posture of a sensible man who has shrugged off the pedagogic mannerisms of his tribe and is

135

engaged in a therapeutic purge of mystification. But what he cannot avoid is speaking down to his audience; he must convert technicalities into ordinary language (which may or may not be salutary) and difficulties must be rendered in terms of the nearest available analogy from commonplace experience (which is very frequently misleading).

The practical point of popularization emerges clearly in the fact that it is very common for works of popularization to be the vehicles for some religious or political message. In physics, for example, this was as true for Fontenelle in the eighteenth century, one of the orginators of the genre, as for Eddington and Jeans in the twentieth. A brilliant popularizer of mathematics like Lancelot Hogben squeezes his subject matter to propagate the conditions for what he regards as a better world. And the recent vogue for popularization in zoology, like an earlier vogue which rested upon sociology, exploits a modern tendency towards social breast-beating. We argued earlier that there is no academic subject which can logically generate religious or political conclusions. It follows that the messages embedded in a great deal of popularization are extraneous to the subject matter with which they purport to deal. The religious scepticism of Fontenelle, the religiosity of Eddington and Jeans, the socialism of Hogben, and the social criticism of people like Vance Packard or Desmond Morris: all of these are opinions which can be held – and have been held – by people entirely unfamiliar with the sciences in which each of these opinions is to be found embedded.

Some abstract accounts of popularization are likely to make it sound indistinguishable from any kind of education. The popularizer, like any expositor, must be able to link his subject matter with the experience of his audience. He must, in other words, make it 'relevant'. But whereas the undergraduate may be assumed ready to cope with difficulties, the general reader will not. Consequently, in popularization the links will have to be short cuts, and the intellectual quality of the popularization is almost precisely a function of how short they are. Popularization is further distinguished by the subsequent behaviour of its readers. The undergraduate is expected to develop into a self-moving inquirer in the subjects he has studied, whereas popularization is in most cases a single and isolated intellectual exercise. Since an audience's approbation plays a big part in the success of a work of popularization, such works tend to confirm what the audience had half been thinking all along; self-satisfaction (which may result from self-flagellation) is the commonest outcome. What works of popularization seem to generate is not a taste for going deeper into a subject, but a taste for reading more popularization.

Popularization encourages the illusion that to be educated is the same thing as to pontificate. It tends to release the prophet usually buried in the breast of most academics. By means of popularization, certain men come to stand for certain academic disciplines: Kenneth Clark stands for art and Desmond Morris for zoology in the same way that C. E. M. Joad and Arnold Toynbee used to stand for philosophy and history respectively. The great popularizer is always a man of ability, though he is not always an outstanding academic contributor to his subject. But whatever the contribution he may have made, the moment he begins to incarnate his subject, he becomes the object of relentless academic sniping from his colleagues, for whom his formulae soon become the very model of unimaginative error, the kind of thing it is their business to keep at bay. This sniping often looks like envy of the successful; sometimes it may be just that. But it also responds to the fact that popularization involves some measure of vulgarization, since simplicity has been achieved at the cost of truth, and the assault on a difficult idea has been abandoned in favour of a gentle climb to a neighbouring cliché. Aside from this kind of specific defect, *any* formulation of an academic truth can only be taken as a starting point for further formulations; the academic world consists in the continuous *process* of tracing out new formulations. To detach any set of these formulations as the *product*

137

of the process is the very model of what is excellent in journalism but debased in scholarship.

These various forms of intellectual journalism cultivate an academic appearance; and as a result they are often judged by academic standards, and inevitably found defective. But it is an error to take them at their own valuation. If we see them as (what in fact they are) practical employments of notions derived from the academic world for the purposes of instruction and entertainment, then they become things in their own right and must be judged differently. Some popularization is brilliant in its own right, and nearly all of it diffuses a certain amount of useful information. Above all, perhaps, popularizers act as liaison officers between the academic worlds, and help to prevent the distinction I am abstractly describing from turning into a rigid barrier between two parts of society. Popularization must, then, be seen as having not academic virtues but rather specific qualities of its own.

These are the qualities of liveliness which make all good journalism significant, entertaining and useful. What journalism itself has taught us to call 'the modern world' is something we enter only by virtue of possessing journalism's own 'knowledgeability'. Just as journalism presses upon schools to supply background rather than to educate, so it also presses upon universities to arrange for undergraduates a kind of cognitive kit of things which Every Modern Man Should Know: scraps of history, a comic strip of the theory of relativity, the Œdipus complex, the gist of Buddhism, the character of a servo-mechanism, the social system, Shakespeare, alienation, the Grail legend, and a thousand other cultural entities which, from time to time, capture the public imagination. Many courses at universities, conceived as broad and general introductions to culture, exhibit many traces of their character as initiations into the world of journalism. Popularization both creates and feeds this desire. It entertains, it is always relevant, and it communicates an exciting sense of participating in man's great cultural adventure. But from an academic point of view this exciting world has serious defects. The categories of journalism are conventional. Reality is caught in a broad-meshed sieve; much slips through and journalism does not tarry to try again. Again, this is why it is entirely at the mercy of the atmosphere of the time. Journalism is a parasitic activity. It can do nothing else but follow in the wake of men who seek to understand from quite other motives than an admiration of knowledgeability. Once a man has built himself a temple in the desert, composed an *oeuvre* which transposes the hopelessness of the human condition into artistic images, explored the seas with strange devices, or found reasons for trying to decipher the traces left by long extinct peoples, then the journalist will follow, and he will explain something like these activities to his fellow mortals. But he will always remain a phototropic nocturnal traveller. He beats a path to the brightest lights. But he lacks illumination of his own.

7 The Ideological Imitation: The Dangers of a Little Learning

Giving an account of ideology – even for the limited purposes involved here – is like trying to fix the outlines of a fog. If we begin, as is commonly done, with some such general formula as that an ideology is an 'action-oriented belief system' then we shall soon find ourselves languishing in the vales of formless abstraction. Let us rather try to build up an account of it by the use of individual detail. Consider the career of the young Karl Marx setting out to make his intellectual fortune early in the nineteenth century. He was a young bourgeois Rhinelander, with a legal and rabbinical background, who very early discovered a taste for intellectual excitements. For what could be more fascinating than to penetrate the mists of appearance (in which most people pass their lives) and to arrive at the firm, clear outlines of reality itself. Such is one version of *furor philosophicus*. It is not the only version, and it is a version evidently close to religious passions. But it can give rise to perfectly genuine understanding. Consider further that this philosophical passion is allied, in Marx, not to a taste for the quiet of contemplation, but to an activist passion which seeks to bring down evil and to enthrone good in the world. Nor was this evil, as Marx saw it, the abstract property of a complex philosophical position. It appeared exemplified before his very eyes in the condition of

140

the poor. To understand the world and to change it have traditionally been thought different endeavours. Who contemplates does not act, and he who acts must abandon contemplation. But ever since the seventeenth century adopted the slogan that knowledge is power, the gap between action and thought seemed to narrow. Marx was not the first to be seized by the illumination that philosophy is power: that a vision of reality could simultaneously be the path to human regeneration. Marx did not long tarry over making this identification, and his statement of the point, jotted down in a hotel room in Cologne in 1845, has become the fervent text of millions of young successors: 'Philosophers have only interpreted the world in various ways. The point is to change it.' There is a fine and dazzling confidence to this, especially to saying *'the* point'. It is a sentence which is a very precise expression of a passion, and ideology is the outcome of that passion.

Marx's passion supplied him with a career: it was a curious career, which involved exile and estrangement, but it can nonetheless be immediately recognized as such. Marx belonged to an ideological class of men whom E. H. Carr has called 'the romantic exiles', and both of Carr's words capture important features of their situation. They were all men who had thrown off any merely calculating attachment to ordinary forms of social advancement; they had embraced poverty and hardship in the name of a master passion. They were lovers in thrall to an idea, and their distant princess was a completely new condition of society. In her service, they eagerly embraced a lifetime of trials and tests. They were, in many ways, a striking and attractive group of men, in whom peaks of heroism and brilliance are matched by valleys of tiresome and petty quarrelling. Many of them, Marx especially, shared not only the romantic tendencies of their time but also its passion for science and technicality. The philosophy by which the world was to be transformed could not look like the more casual wisdom of the past. It required an apparatus of technicality to turn it into a suitably im-

141

pressive piece of esoteric knowledge. Ironically enough, the very word 'ideology' has been vulgarized in this way and come to mean any kind of political principle. The profession of ideologist included, then, a considerable equipment of more or less technical information, and entry to the profession was by way of mastering a body of appropriate knowledge. Generally, this was a profession adopted by young men in countries where opportunities for orthodox political careers were slight or non-existent. They scorned the civil service (for which their education equipped them) and they scorned trade. They took up conspiracy, and they gave an example which has in the last century spread all over the world. In the early stages the profession prospered on the edges of respectable society, and the status of its practitioners was in some respect not unlike that of the Hebrew prophets of the Old Testament. But with growing opportunity, the profession became more respectable, and ideologists could be seen as divided into activist and contemplative types. Marx belonged to the contemplative kind of ideologist, and it is this type which has produced the body of knowledge which stands as a challenge to and an imitation of the academic world.

Marxism, for example, has become ramified in such a way that each academic subject has its 'Marxist' shadow: this matching ranges all the way from economics and politics to physics and genetics. Mostly, ideologies such as nationalism or racialism have little claim to be taken seriously in academic terms, but in Marxism we have a case of something that stands four-square as claiming intellectual equality with, indeed superiority to, what is otherwise taught in universities. If this claim is accepted, then Marxist assertions about economics and other subjects must be taken as an addition to the scope of academic inquiry. Now there can be no doubt that many of the assertions made in Marxist writings may be taken academically as hypotheses: and this is hardly surprising, since most of them had earlier been taken from academic writing. This means that there is some substance in the Marxist claim to be participating in the attempt to understand the world. This claim is also made by other ideologies; but by and large, we may take Marxism as by far the most inventive and elaborate (as well as current) of ideologies, and our conclusion about it may stand as a general conclusion about the intellectual status of any ideology.

The problem of an ideologist is to create a 'philosophy' (which may be any apparently academic form of knowledge) which is simultaneously a guide to action. Such a combination would seem to be inherently impossible. In making a moral or political decision, we commonly distinguish between the facts of the case and the possible courses of action open to us. If we are being rational, we marshal arguments favouring or opposing the various courses of action, and make our decision according to the strongest case. One important presupposition of this kind of activity of choosing is that the outcome of our deliberations is essentially indeterminate. It could not be predicted (though it might be successfully forecast). We assume, in other words, that we are genuinely free; but most ideologies have been, for reasons which will emerge, hostile to this assumption. But so long as we accept the view that human beings are free moral agents, then we are committed to distinguishing between an understanding of the world and a policy for dealing with it. This is the structure of practical thought which will be found among the Athenians discussing how to treat the Melian rebels, Hamlet contemplating suicide, the Romans considering who should command the armies that would have to deal with Hannibal, Caesar at the Rubicon, or the British considering what course of action to take after the fall of France. Now in these traditional terms a philosophy which simultaneously tells us what to do is an impossibility. For there is no logical way in which a description can generate a prescription.

But logic, of course, is not the point. Oliver Wendell Holmes, in a famous example, denied that the right to freedom of speech covered the man who cried 'Fire!' in a crowded theatre. For this descriptive statement, combined

143

with the audience's instinct for not being burned alive, would generate the highly practical (and disastrous) policy of rushing the exits. Orators have always known that explicit advocacy and justification could very largely be replaced by a sufficiently skilful description of the world. But this technical possibility remained of interest only to the virtuoso rhetorician until the moment came when there might be both reason to pretend that advocacy was something else, and an audience simple enough to be persuaded of it. The first thing that must be done in constructing an ideology is, then, to purge it of all explicit advocacy or justification. For the crucial distinction between a description and a prescription is that while the former may be more or less conclusively supported by evidence, the latter remains eternally powerless against the obdurate. An ideologist may immediately be identified as a political writer who seeks to make his arguments appear entirely academic, and who must gain all his political effects by an apparatus of selective description.

The simplest way of understanding the central features of this technical innovation is to consider one of the simplest attributes of language. In everyday discourse, we all use easily and fluently words which simply point to objects in the world, or to aspects of those objects (hat, tree, house, green, hard, etc); and words which indicate our attitude to things (good, bad, horrible, disgusting); and words which combine these two functions (blackguard, tyrant, terrorist, rebel). Now it is obvious that the first class of words may be useful in describing the world, but will never guide us in action; and that the second class of words will guide our attitudes, but will not tell us very much. If we are to solve the ideologist's problem, which is to construct a body of knowledge which will also guide us in action, then we must make use of the third class of words, which simultaneously describe and guide our emotions. But in academic terms, such words are recognized as dangerous to the understanding. To talk academically is, very strictly, to purge one's discourse of words of this very kind. The trick of constructing a successful ideology is to coin new technical terms which operate as logical amphibians in this third manner.

Hence it is that the categories of ideology – such as 'revolution', 'proletariat', 'imperialist', 'class war', 'race', 'decadence', 'progress', 'reaction', and the rest – are categories of practice. They betray a bastard parentage: the mother is a thought, sometimes a respectably academic thought, but the father is a passion, and often one of the nastier passions – hatred, greed, envy or revenge. It is impossible to use even the thin cognitive content of these terms without taking up an attitude towards whatever is imagined in connection with them. And since they have been created in response to practical questions, they cannot, in their unpurged state, be used in the framing or answering of academic questions. Academically speaking they are feeble, though this feebleness is sometimes obscured by the ideological disposition towards abusive labelling as a substitute for thought. The categories of ideology determine our attitude to, not our understanding of, the world; and they have the important practical convenience of bringing to an end any chain of inquiry. They are preludes either to action, or to the adoption of an attitude (which is a kind of action); and thereafter the appropriate response to them is to search for *confirmations* of the act or the attitude. For once we have acted, what we most want is to be shown to have acted rightly.

An ideology is, then, a description of the world, designed to determine action, couched in apparently academic technicalities which nonetheless contain signals – which are necessarily unsubtle – of the attitude we should adopt. The explanatory force of ideologies depends upon the extent to which we can actually identify, in the world at large, entities corresponding to what the ideology describes. Thus (to continue using Marxism as our model of an ideology) if we can identify people as bourgeois and proletarian, then we shall find Marxism to that extent plausible. And the plausibility of this distinction depends upon the fact that we do dis-

145

tinguish in practical terms between the rich and the poor. Marxist ideology depends for much of its political influence upon transposing our sympathy for the poor into an attitude towards the technical concept of the 'proletariat', a concept which plays an important part in the technicalities of Marxist thinking. But as with all abstractions, the concept of 'proletariat' is intellectually impressive and useful to precisely the extent that it masks out the real diversity of the actual poor. For some of the desires and strivings of those who are actually poor have been transposed, in this ideological thought, into the *defining* characteristics of the proletariat. Others of these defining characteristics have been invented. Any actually poor person will also be a member of a state; he will have a religion, and a race, and colour, and he will also have a personal temperament. What may be confidently predicated of proletarians is likely to be quite false of actually poor people; and this has proved to be the case on many occasions most notably when the actually poor, who had (so Marxists had been patiently explaining to them) no homeland, did in fact actually respond to the call of defending their homelands in 1914. The proletariat is, of course, a peculiarly vulnerable ideological concept, and may be easily recognized as a fantasy composed by intellectuals ambitious to play a role in politics. It has very frequently gone wrong in practice. But in its vulnerability it merely illustrates an important logical defect of all ideological terms: that once 'interests' in what we may naively call the real world have been transposed into 'defining characteristics' in ideological theory, then the attempt at a real understanding of the world has been abandoned in favour of a preferred fantasy.

The traditional understanding of deliberative thinking divides the world into things and agents. Some such dualism, whether it be mind and matter or the natural and the human spheres, runs right through Western philosophy up to modern times. Ideological writing reduces this dualistic understanding of human action to a single world of objects to be described. It thus necessarily denies the reality of deliberation. The business of human choosing has to be seen as merely a superficial peculiarity of minds which, if fully understood, would not be logically distinct from a natural event. Thus choices may be labelled as 'bourgeois' and 'proletarian', and the choice a man actually makes merely reveals a real character which had been there all the time. The only imponderability results from ignorance. Choices are exhibited, in ideological thinking, as the 'products' of some such social factor as nation, race or class. Professor Tucker, in commenting upon Marx's use of the expression 'under our very eyes', quotes him, in a typical utterance, as saying that it 'is not a matter of bringing some utopian system or other into being, but of consciously participating in the historical revolutionary process of society which is taking place before our very eyes'.[1] The distinction between an ideology and other forms of political thought may be precisely measured, within Marxism, by the very different connotations of 'utopianism' and 'historical processes'. Utopianism means the advocacy of desirabilities which take no account of historical possibility, but for all its defects it is a way of recognizing that men have real options in politics. It is the most intellectually vulnerable form of that recognition, which is, of course, why Marx chose that name to cover – and to cover with obloquy – all versions of it. No one, on the other hand, has the option of resisting a historical process. If they even make the attempt, they will infallibly be consigned to what Trotsky (describing his Menshevik opponents) once called 'the dustbin of history'. Any such doctrine, by attuning men's actions with grand universal forces, gives an ideology enormous persuasive power. But it also severs an ideology irredeemably from the academic world.

Paradoxically, the attempt to purge political discourse of its evaluative elements by transposing them into an academic key is to produce that most emotion-drenched of all artistic forms, a melodrama. Ideology is political thought on the loosest possible rein, and it will often include large

[1] Robert Tucker, *Philosophy and Myth in Karl Marx*, Cambridge 1961, p. 225.

chunks of descriptive and philosophical material; but it is distinguished by the fact that all of this material clearly subserves a single simple design, and that design is melodramatic. This is the reason why the central concept of an ideology is the concept of a struggle, and that the terms of this struggle are always fundamentally moral entities. Marx himself reveals this clearly in the Manifesto, the popular work in which the design of his writing is at its most academically defenceless, when he writes: 'Freeman and slave, patrician and plebeian, lord and serf, guild-master and journeyman, in a word, oppressor and oppressed ...' The hinge of ideological thought is the identification of a process, which is an object of scientific inquiry, with a struggle, which is a moral encounter between human beings. This hinge allows the ideologist to play the moralist or the scientist according to convenience. It also allows him the option of refusing to take his critics seriously, by simply writing them off as mere terms of the historical process. Marx, for example, is able to treat Proudhon with ineffable superiority by dismissing him as a 'petit-bourgeois.'[2] This particular ideological device was developed by Marx into the *theory* of ideology. All inconvenient disagreement is dismissed by allocation to some supposed social source. This is a matter of such importance that we shall return to it in the next chapter.

The view that I am taking, then, is that an ideology is a form of pseudo-science whose design is determined by its political character. The examples I have been using are all Marxist. The reason for this is that Marxism has been developed with considerable intelligence and has contributed to the body of ideological thinking many of its most commonly employed resources. But our analysis of ideology would not vary greatly if we turned to Houston Stewart Chamberlain interpreting European history in terms of the struggle between the Jewish and Aryan races, or the similar

[2] Consider, for example, the First Observation in chapter 2 of *The Poverty of Philosophy*, where the game of academic one-upmanship is played with quite masterly skill.

148

view, laced with fragments of Darwinism, found in *Mein Kampf*; or, indeed, any of the nationalist writing currently being produced by champions of the 'underdeveloped' world in their struggle against colonialism and imperialism. It should be emphasized that ideological thinking is now a very common form of political and moral self-expression amongst modern men. A peculiarly pure example of ideological thinking as the form that myth takes in modern societies would be the essay called 'The Primaeval Mitosis' in which the Black Power theorist Eldridge Cleaver interprets social and racial conflict in terms of the evolution of human types which he calls Omnipotent Administrator, Supermasculine Menial, Ultrafeminines and Amazons. In this case, as in many, the various pure forms of ideology are scrambled together, so that the 'fundamental struggle' involves race, class, sex, nation and any other abstraction that happens to come to hand. Here, also, a theory of human evolution constitutes the basic structure of the variation. It would be difficult to imagine a fully developed ideology which did not employ a theory of evolution, for an ideology must always explain how we came to our present situation; and to do this in intellectual terms inevitably involves positing stages of growth.

The borderline between ideological thinking and other forms of political discourse is often difficult to draw, but it is a mistake to avoid this problem by taking any 'ism' to be an ideology. Indeed, most 'isms' describe a miscellany of political beliefs, many of which are not properly ideological at all. Consider the case of a man who believed that unrestricted commercial competition stunts human life, and that it would be a good thing if democratic governments were to take over large industries by nationalizing them. Such a man would clearly be a socialist, but he would not be, in any interesting sense, an ideologist. For when asked to support his view he would produce general arguments appealing to desirability and principle, and he would recognize the existence of arguments against what he supported. But if, on the other hand, like Marx, he derived socialist attitudes from what purported to be an academic or scientific analysis of history, then it would make sense to treat him as an ideologist; for clearly the logic of this latter position is different. Similarly, most liberals are people who believe in the superiority of freedom of speech and the rule of law; this does not make them ideologists. But if they supported this policy by appealing to Darwin's theory of evolution, and thus treating competition between firms for business, and between men for jobs, as the necessary way of ensuring the survival of the fittest and the progress of mankind, then the introduction of ideological thinking would have begun. The introduction of an ideological principle into political thinking is like the presence of a magnet amongst iron filings. Each fact becomes a confirmation and they cluster together in a unity and design which traditional political thinking does not have.

The history of ideological thinking is not our direct concern. It is worth noting, however, that ideology emerged out of a particular episode in the conflict between the academic and the practical worlds as we have already discussed it. The general hope which inspires ideological thinking – that there exists an accessible body of knowledge by which human decisions might be infallibly determined – is as old as Plato. The *Republic* is a classical statement of the view. But the hopes of actually achieving it were given a great fillip in the seventeenth century when both technology and the body of theory exploring its possibilities vastly expanded. This led directly to the modern hope that just as knowledge helped man to control nature, so social knowledge would allow him to control his moral and political destiny. Since human history appeared to be little more than a list of follies and crimes, this was obviously a hope worth taking seriously. In the course of the seventeenth and eighteenth centuries the conviction grew among many educated men that the cause of human misery was not original sin but the absence of reason from much human behaviour. As this view was developed, it led to the conclusion that reason was absent from political affairs because its place had been usurped by authority. It had been Hobbes who produced in the *Leviathan* a brilliant account of authority as necessary in human affairs because the reasons for doing any particular act were never conclusive. Later thinkers wrote this off as a mere apology for absolutism, and took the view that the ideal political community would be one in which political decisions were taken entirely on rational grounds and were obeyed for the same reason. If this could be achieved, then political life would indeed be transformed. This line of thought was widely cultivated amongst the *philosophes* in France. It sought to replace authority by reason, especially in politics. What it in fact achieved was to transfer authority away from traditional powers to those who spoke in what could be passed off as philosophical or academic language. By a collection of curious circumstances, academic language became the language of authority, which necessitated the pretence that no authority was really being exercised at all. Among some French Revolutionaries, who were the first to put this new invention into practice, a belief in their own rationality was such that anyone who disagreed with them had to be understood as a scoundrel. Such people were treated appropriately. It is one of the sadder ironies of human history, but one very relevant to the emergence of ideological thinking, that a series of movements which were designed to replace force and violence in human affairs by reason and persuasion has almost always succeeded in augmenting the shedding of blood.

In some such way as this, then, ideological thinking came to dominate the modern world, but it only began to attain its present cacophonous pitch about the middle of the nineteenth century, when many doctrines of social evolution suddenly appeared to promise a new dawn of rationality. Each new doctrine was brought forth from a variety of motives, but each promised release from confusion, division, hatred, war and the inflictions of governments. Since that time, ideological thinking has become an inevitable form of self-expression, and ideologies have borrowed devices and arguments from each other to such an extent that it is hard to distinguish one from another. Even the great central tradition of Marxism has been revised, regenerated, corrected, negated and synthesized almost out of recognition. Nevertheless, the claim that any ideology makes to an importance beyond that of other doctrines depends on the extent to which it appears as either genuinely academic or (to take an alternative we shall have to consider in the next section) actually superior to the thinking that goes on in universities. And in this respect, Marxism must again be granted a pre-eminence. What we must next do, then, is to consider Marxism as a form of knowledge. Let us, however, emphasize one crucial point: that even if we should discover that Marxism has no academic validity whatever, it would not in any way imply that the practical aims espoused by Marxists are defective. The desirability or otherwise of the revolutionary transformation of society and the expropriation of the expropriators would remain as before, neither better nor worse.

We noted earlier that Marxism stood for a position on most academic subjects, but it would be tedious and unprofitable to go through them all in order to estimate the validity of their Marxist shadows. What we need to consider is Marxism as a philosophy, paying attention on the way to some of its historical and scientific aspects.

Just as Marx the economist went into business with capital borrowed from Adam Smith and Ricardo, so Marx the philosopher began with what he got from Hegel. And while Hegel is a philosopher who can still arouse strong passions in the breasts of modest Anglo-Saxon philosophers, we need not doubt that he was a respectably academic source. But then, Marx did not go on to become a Hegelian philosopher. For one thing, he claimed to 'stand Hegel on his feet'. In other words, he became a materialist. But there are no actual arguments for materialism in Marx. We simply find it taken for granted that the world is real, and that the ideas of previous philosophers have merely reflected, in a distorted fashion, the condition of the society in which they lived. Philosophy, in a justly celebrated image, is to Marxist practice as onanism is to sexual intercourse. This taking of common sense for granted is not philosophy, but a refusal to philosophize. And as such, it may be deliberate. For there is one reading of Hegel's philosophy[3] which takes it to be not one philosophy among others, but the culmination of man's constant endeavour to attain the full self-consciousness of the human spirit. On this view, the work of philosophy ended when it produced the dialectical understanding of reality, and all that was needed was the small adjustment to materialism given by Marx. The task of mankind then ceases to be that of philosophy (which is to attain full self-consciousness) and becomes that of taking philosophy into the world. The mind has at last brought forth reason; now reason must change the world. Such would seem to be the message of the XIth Thesis on Feuerbach.[4] This view of Hegel, let it be added, is not the one widely held by academic students of his philosophy today, and it would indeed seem to be a rather simple-minded view of the thought of so subtle a man as Hegel. But it is easy to see that its missionary element might appeal to an eager disciple.

Marx the philosopher, then, was a materialist who used the Hegelian dialectical logic. He produced a quantity of philosophical argument during the 1840s, and then, apart

---

[3] Herbert Marcuse, *Reason and Revolution*, Oxford 1941.

[4] And also of the IVth thesis, where Marx argues that Feuerbach, in revealing religious beliefs as merely projections of the social realm, had not gone on to realise the 'self-contradictoriness' of that social realm. 'The latter must itself, therefore, first be understood in its contradictions and then, by the removal of the contradiction, revolutionised in practice. Thus, for instance, once the earthly family is discovered to be the secret of the holy family, the former must then itself be criticised in theory and revolutionised in practice.' Whoever can capture, in reading these three short pages, the intellectual excitement of seeing through the veils of appearance to the social reality of existence will have understood the psychological power of ideological thinking.

Imitations of the Academic

from the long-unpublished *Grundrisse* (which does not seem to have broken new philosophical ground), he wrote virtually nothing on philosophy thereafter. His French philosophical exponent, Louis Althusser, sees this as a problem, and goes on to produce an elaborate theory of it. All philosophies, Althusser argues, depend upon the discovery of 'continents' of knowledge; and Marx's philosophical silence is caused by the fact that he was working, from *The German Ideology* onwards, towards the construction of a new continent of knowledge called the science of history.[5] Here, as often, Althusser takes the bull by the horns, and advances Marx's claims to philosophical eminence upon his denunciation of philosophy as being mere ideology, as 'a hallucination and mystification, or to go further, as a dream, manufactured from what I shall call the day's residues of the real history of concrete men, day's residues endowed with a purely imaginary existence in which the order of things is inverted'.[6]

In saying this, Althusser is indeed faithful to Marx. This is clear if we try to catch the drift of what Marx was saying in *The German Ideology*. To catch this drift is a somewhat dangerous exercise, because *The German Ideology* is, like everything Marx wrote at that time, deeply involved with highly parochial controversies current among the Young Hegelians. Leaving this proviso aside, however, we may observe the adumbration of a theory which was to have great currency:

Hitherto men have constantly made up for themselves false conceptions about themselves, about what they are and what they ought to be.... The phantoms of their brains have gained the mastery over them.... It has not occurred to any one of these philosophers to inquire into the connection of German philosophy with German reality, the relation of their criticism to their own

[5] Louis Althusser. *Lenin and Philosophy and other essays*, London 1971, pp. 40–1.
[6] *Ibid.*, p. 41.

154

material surroundings. . . . The first premise of all human history is, of course, the existence of living human individuals . . .[7]

These remarks from the first few pages indicate pretty clearly the drift of the argument. It can best be compared with the occasion on which Dr Johnson, asked about his view of Bishop Berkeley's idealist philosophy, kicked a nearby stone to emphasize his sense of reality, and remarked: 'I refute it *thus*.' The case amounts, in other words, to an appeal away from Hegel's idealism to the commonsense view that reality consists in human beings, with their material conditions of life, thinking thoughts. Philosophically, this merely begs the question. Philosophy is, among other things, the question: 'What is reality?' To assume that we already know is to refuse to philosophize. It is, indeed, an available human option. But it does not generate a philosophy.

Still, our concern is not to estimate the validity of Marxist philosophy but to estimate its relation to academic inquiry. And even the quick sketch we have so far provided allows us to observe something which is true not only of Marx but of the wider field of ideologies with which we are concerned. Some philosophizing is unavoidable in ideological thinking (as in the thinking of all intellectual ventures which are, in our broad sense, religious) because philosophy constitutes a form of 'last word' upon the human situation. Philosophers are concerned with human understanding, and their common procedure is to examine the validity of different forms of human understanding – the practical, the religious, the scientific, the historical, and indeed that of philosophy itself. That which examines is, in an important sense, superior to that which is examined. Philosophy thus constitutes an area which might, and indeed will, attempt to have the last word

[7] R. Pascal (ed.), *The German Ideology*, London 1938, pp. 1–6. If this terminology of 'catching the drift' should irritate the reader, I can only say that there does not seem to me to be a coherent argument to report. It is a highly rhetorical production, in which Marx's former colleagues are denounced as charlatans, fakes and dealers in shoddy philosophical goods. Marx seems to have been very wise in what he chose to publish and in what he did not.

about any ideological theory. Now philosophical or academic criticism of any kind of human belief is in practice embarrassing, and even believers with no serious academic pretensions, such as fundamentalist Biblical sects, are forced to formulate some kind of attitude to academics who regard their beliefs as ridiculous. But the case of ideologies is different from that of religious sects, for it is a defining characteristic of an ideology that it must pretend to *academic* superiority. All ideologies are based upon some perception which first arose in academic inquiry. Consequently, academic criticism is peculiarly damaging to ideologies, and they all take great pains to deal with it.

Certain aspects of this response to academic criticism must be considered in the next section. But the central point of what Marx has to say about philosophy can be indicated immediately. Marx realized that philosophy need not be allowed to monopolize the 'last word' upon human understanding. For it is obviously the case that any philosopher, contemplating the validity and grades of human knowledge, will be located at some point in time, and that others will come after him. Therefore, in one sense, it is history and the passage of time which always has the last word. Philosophies are refuted because time, which takes survey of all the world, will *not* have a stop. Or, alternatively, any philosopher is a social animal, may be located within a social structure and may thus be at least undermined if he is presented as playing some socially determined role. One need not bother with the small print of metaphysics if idealism, for example, can be comprehensively dismissed as 'bourgeois apologetics'. This position is not affected by the fact that meanwhile the philosophers will be taking to pieces the forms of inquiry exemplified by history and sociology, and that the battle for the 'last word' goes on forever. To recognize that it does so is one of the fundamental operative assumptions of the academic world. To assume that there must be some definitive 'last word' is equally to make the fundamental claim that must be made by any religion. If this is true, then it follows that Marx's simple reduction of philosophy to social circumstance must be taken as a practical device.

This conclusion is confirmed if we consider the tone of voice in which Marx, and indeed most Marxists, write. It is a dogmatic tone, full of scornful confidence and equipped with an abundance of abusive labels with which to castigate those who have the temerity to disagree. There is no sense of the hypothetical, no feeling for the cooperative enterprise of a conversation, and above all not the slightest recognition that to be wrong is an ordinary hazard of thought, and that therefore one may have to give up some cherished theory. For Marx to abandon a doctrine is to bleed. He fights against the necessity of doing so with every rhetorical weapon at his command: abuse, sarcasm, equivocation and contempt. And this example has been followed by Marxists ever since: even the gentler Engels succumbed. Terms like 'blockhead', 'charlatan', 'petit-bourgeois' and 'craven' abound. A good deal of Marxism sounds like a bad-tempered schoolmaster with a class full of blockheads.

Is this abuse merely an unfortunate continental habit of mind, or does it supply us with a clue to the real character of the philosophizing which occurs in ideological thinking? It is true that German philosophers have often tended to abuse each other, but they do in general take each other's arguments seriously. In Marxist philosophy, the question is usually begged by abusing those who disagree. Althusser is entirely within the tradition when he writes:

Philosophy teachers are teachers, i.e., intellectuals employed in a given education system and subject to that system performing, as a mass, the social function of inculcating the 'values of the ruling ideology'.... Philosophers are intellectuals and therefore petty bourgeois, subject as a mass to bourgeois and petty-bourgeois ideology.... This situation, shared by those petty-bourgeois intellectuals, the philosophy teachers, and by the philosophy they teach or reproduce in their own individual form, does not mean that it is impossible for certain intellectuals to escape the constraints that dominate the mass of intellectuals, and, if philosophers, to adhere to a materialist philosophy and a revolutionary theory.[8]

Skating on thin ice is one thing, but this is walking on water. Whoever rejects Marxism is flicked aside as 'constrained by the system'. Whoever accepts it is flattered as an intrepid and liberated thinker. It takes a very gullible reader indeed to fall in with an invitation of this kind. The sophistry here is the same as the sophistry which is writ large throughout *The German Ideology*. Its technical name is *ignoratio elenchi*, but it is more popularly known as bluff. In the free-for-all of ideological discussion, it no doubt takes a trick or two. But it will be clear from the argument that we have presented that it represents the abandonment of the academic attempt to understand in favour of the practical attempt at domination.

Nor is this last assertion regarded as particularly disreputable in ideological circles. M. Althusser is happy to embrace it directly: 'Once I had a better understanding of Marxist-Leninist politics, I began to have a passion for philosophy *too*, for at last I began to understand the great thesis of *Marx, Lenin* and *Gramsci*: that philosophy is fundamentally *political*.'[9] This view merely states what we may confidently take to be the central assertion of any ideology: that the reality of the world is constituted of a single fundamental struggle, and the meaning of absolutely everything must be seen in relation to that struggle. To align oneself on the correct side of that struggle is, to use appropriately religious language, 'the one thing needful'. Once this view has been accepted (and since it is a metaphysical view which asserts the fundamental character of reality, and which therefore determines rather than responds to evidence, its acceptance can only be a leap of faith), then it follows that all forms of understanding can only be validated in terms of that struggle. This means, in the case of

[8] Althusser, pp. 67–8.
[9] Althusser, p. 15. The emphasis is in the text.

universities, that, to the extent that academic criticism appears to run counter to ideological assertion, it can be *nothing else but* the defensive ratiocination of the evil side of the struggle. Ideologists, whose intellectual identity owes so much to academic models, have not hesitated to take the extreme view that academic inquiry is itself nothing but the ideology of the ruling class. If this were true, it would be entirely fatal to the argument we have been presenting. We must now turn to passing in review the arguments commonly adduced for it.

8 Is the Academic World Itself Ideological?

This question can only be approached if we keep clearly in mind the two almost diametrically opposite meanings of the term 'ideology'. As we have used it, 'ideology' signifies any one of those intellectualized political doctrines which have become current in the last two centuries. Nationalism, Communism, Populism, and Consciencism would be examples of ideologies in this sense of the term. Such is the way in which it is most commonly used. But an adherent of any of these doctrines does not regard himself as merely one among others; rather, he is the possessor of an important and unique truth, scientifically demonstrable, and fighting for its diffusion against vested interest and the obscurantist intellectual defences of an established order. As we have seen, this vision of the ideologist's situation was elaborately stated in *The German Ideology*, but a clearer version of the doctrine appears much later, in 1859, in one of those highly-compressed summaries of his thinking of which Marx was a master. In the Preface he wrote to the *Contribution to a Critique of Political Economy* Marx wrote that: 'It is not the consciousness of men that determines their being, but, on the contrary, their social being that determines their consciousness.' This famous sentence brilliantly sums up the central argument of Marxism, and was developed into a distinction between 'the economic conditions of production, which can be determined with the precision of natural science' and 'the legal, political, religious, aesthetic or philosophic – in short, ideological forms in which men become conscious of this conflict and fight it out'.[1] There is nothing in this theory to suggest that universities are in any way immune from this universal social determination. Indeed, Marx was perfectly happy to advance boldly to the assertion that they were not.

It is, then, one of the confusing eccentricities of this field of inquiry that Marxism is both itself an ideology, since it is an intellectualized political doctrine, and also not an ideology, since it is scientific socialism struggling to destroy the beliefs by which capitalism justifies itself. Marxism is thus both ideology and science, depending on how we use the words. Marx himself, however, simply declared his own doctrine to be science and regarded whatever opposed it as ideology. In the same Preface from which we have been quoting, Marx describes how in 1845 he and Engels settled in Brussels, and 'resolved to work out in common the opposition of our view to the ideological view of German philosophy, in fact, to settle accounts with our erstwhile philosophical conscience'.[2]

Marx believed that his intellectual opponents were all tainted by the distortions of the system, while he himself had broken through to truth. This was taken for granted. It was nowhere argued. Critics of Marxism have commonly turned Marx's own theory against him, pointing out that he too has a social location, and his thought too must be distorted. Marxism is not, however, entirely helpless before the charge that it illicitly excludes itself from the laws of social determination upon which it insists so rigorously for others. Ideology, as it appears in Marxist thought, describes a distortion in thought resulting from the fact that in any class-divided society, thinkers have available to them only a limited because class-bound point of view. But if it is the

[1] The Preface is frequently reprinted. See Marx and Engels, *op. cit.* vol. I, p. 327.
[2] *Ibid.*, p. 330.

case that Marxism *is* the ideology of the proletariat, and if it is also the case that the proletariat is about to transform capitalist society and become the entirety of the post-revolutionary society, then the thoughts of the proletariat could plausibly be taken to represent a total rather than a fragmentary point of view. Such an argument is commonly employed, and obviously attractive. It has, however, the disadvantage of begging the question: for it asserts that if Marxism is right (in its assertions and predictions) then Marxism is in possession of the truth.

Part of the difficulty of this subject is caused by uncertainty about the status we should accord to Marx's doctrine of ideology. It has the obvious practical use of being a device by which the arguments of opponents may be ruled out of court as being merely (to use a phrase from *The German Ideology*) 'echoes of the life-process'.[3] The theory of ideology is obviously first cousin to the common rhetorical device of refusing to argue the explicit issue with an opponent, and attempting to devalue what he has to say by imputing to him either disreputable motives or some hidden interest of which he is 'stooge' or 'spokesman'. The actual effect of the theory of ideology is, then, to focus attention upon the practical, in this case the political, aspect of any controversy. And since this aspect is always uppermost in the mind of ideologists, it is easy to understand why the theory has been taken over by all political doctrines which regard themselves as being in possession of a unique revelation of truth.

There is nothing in either Marx's tone or in his argument to suggest that he wishes to advance the theory of ideology as a purely academic explanation of the diversity of social beliefs. But he has had successors who have treated the argument in this way, and who have brought forth a genuinely academic subject called the sociology of knowledge. It is certainly plausible to look for clusterings of beliefs in specific social locations, though the results of doing so have not lived up to the hopes of those most enthusiastic about this branch

[3] R. Pascal (ed.), *The German Ideology*, London 1938, p. 14.

of inquiry. For even this respectably academic version of the theory of ideology cannot solve its evident logical confusion : that if beliefs are radically defective *by virtue of* their social origin, then, either truth is unattainable, or if we did attain it, we should have no way of knowing that we had. Alternatively, if the discovery of truths is a possible social activity, then the theory of ideology (which is itself asserted as a truth) must give way to a few feeble comments upon the 'naturalness' or 'appropriateness' of some beliefs to some classes of people.

It is, however, along the broad avenue of the theory of ideology that critics have advanced in attacking the university as being nothing much more than the intellectual wing of the ruling class. All academic teaching, on this view, contains false perspectives which obscure the truth about the world we live in. Such is the argument whose details we must now consider.

As to much of the detail, we must begin by confessing that the charge is often only too true. The practical world has invested many of the suburbs of Academe; it has left its traces nearly everywhere. 'Does academic freedom give a faculty member the right to teach a course in riot-control?'[4] demands a typical radical voice. And although the tone of the rhetorical question and the mention of academic freedom are there to suggest the additional view that no one, anywhere, ought to teach such a subject, one cannot but agree that riot-control is indeed the very paradigm of a subject that has no place whatever in universities. Some people, it is true, see this particular condition of universities not as a falling away but as a portent of the proper evolution of universities. They will become the brain centres of modern society. It is clear that if they do they will cease to be universities in the sense that I have been describing. Up to a point such intrusions of practicality need not be taken too seriously; indeed, it may be suggested that they constitute a kind of homeo-

[4] Alan Wolfe, 'The Professional Mystique' in Marvin Surkin and Alan Wolfe (eds), *An End to Political Science*, New York 1970, p. 292.

pathic remedy for their own disease. The proximity of the practical is often an incitement to academics to gather the tatters of their own identity more closely around them. But in the context of our present question, these traces of the practical are an embarrassment, because they would seem to confirm the ideologist's argument that universities are *systematically* involved in the controversies of the practical world.

I propose now to pass in review the typical arguments in favour of this view; and since it is important that we do not waste our time on straw men, I shall take actual and (I should argue) typical statements of these arguments as a focus for discussion. Let us begin by considering a short and relatively popular argument which exhibits most of the characteristics of the line of thought I am concerned with. As soon as questions about what goes into an academic curriculum and what is left out are raised (so argues Mr Anthony Arblaster) 'whatever the intentions of the questioners may be, ideological issues are brought into the discussion'. As we shall see, bold universals about the utter inescapability of ideological questions have become small change in this kind of educational discussion. But it is not only purposes which are thought ideological:

> The shape of individual areas of study and the manner in which they are taught have been moulded in a similar way. This is most easily perceived in the human and social studies. There are, for example, clearly conservative implications in the basic assumption on which so much contemporary linguistic philosophy is founded: that the job of the philosopher is not to invent new concepts or theories but simply to describe and analyze existing usages.[5]

This view is then exemplified by a well-known passage from J. L. Austin:

> Our common stock of words embodies all the distinctions men have found worth drawing, and the connexions they have found

[5] Anthony Arblaster, 'Education and Ideology', in David Rubinstein and Colin Stoneman (eds), *Education for Democracy*, London 1970, pp. 50–1.

worth making, in the lifetimes of many generations: these surely are likely to be more numerous, more sound ... and more subtle ... than any that you or I are likely to think up in our armchairs of an afternoon.

On this passage, Mr Arblaster comments:

To others of us it is at least equally reasonable to think that new and unfamiliar experiences or ways of seeing the world and human nature may require the formulation of new concepts and new theories, rather than efforts to cram them into old and established categories.

This argument is typical of an entire genre in its combination of a bold universal statement of the doctrine, combined with an almost insolently inapposite fragment of support. The feebleness of that support can be exhibited in a variety of ways. One way is simply to read on a few more pages into Austin's argument, where we find a passage demonstrating clearly that Arblaster's argument is a misunderstanding of what Austin meant:

Certainly ordinary language has no claim to be the last word, if there is such a thing. It embodies, indeed, something better than the metaphysics of the Stone Age, namely, as was said, the inherited experience and acumen of many generations of men. But then, that acumen has been concentrated primarily upon the practical business of life ... it is likely enough to be not the best way of arranging things if our interests are more extensive or intellectual than the ordinary. . . . Certainly, then, ordinary language is *not* the last word: in principle it can everywhere be supplemented and improved upon and superseded. Only remember, it *is* the *first* word.[6]

But even without this elucidation, a second thought about the original passage will cause the argument to crumble. For, using the word 'implication' in any serious sense, what actually *is* implied about politics in it? Where is the radical or revolutionary programme that is stopped in its tracks by

[6] 'A Plea For Excuses' in *Collected Papers*, Oxford 1970, p. 185 (italics in text).

the suggestion that ordinary language contains huge and untapped resources of meaning which are obliterated by the habit of inventing new bits of intellectual jargon every time a thought occurs or an experience is construed? There are, in fact, no political implications in the passage whatever. Thirdly, even if it were true (and more adroitly chosen examples could be adduced to illustrate) that some philosopher had made some political remark, what then follows? Merely that academic argument is sometimes bad and irrelevant, and that practical pressures distort academic thinking. The solution would be for other academics to criticise it, not as evidence of a pervasive ideologicality, but more relevantly, as bad argument. And whether Austin has been caught out in bad argument or not, Mr Arblaster has to go on to admit that critics like Herbert Marcuse and Ernest Gellner (to name but two) have thought they detected serious inadequacies in linguistic philosophy, and have criticized it extensively. This admission being embarrassing for the case he is presenting, he attempts to salvage a little plausibility by referring to Marcuse and Gellner as 'outsiders'. Since both have had successful academic careers, it is difficult to see why he does so.

It may well be objected that this is to take a sledgehammer to a peanut. Perhaps that is so. But what we are dealing with here is not really academic argument, but a form of political propaganda in disguise. And it is a fact of persuasive life that mere repetition is itself a value; further, in this case, what is repeated is a bold universal with a sufficient patina of profundity for it to be passed from mouth to mouth and page to page as a fragment of unchallengeable wisdom. It can only be met by a thorough and patient review of each detail of the mosaic of supportive argument.

In many cases, what we encounter is no more than the statement of a temperamental preference. When we are told that 'To plead for reason, detachment, objectivity or patience in the face of abject poverty, political repression,

and napalmed women and children is absurd'⁷ we may well
recognize a sense of practical urgencies to be admired; but
we must also recognize that the world has always contained
things to be reformed, and always will. To postpone objectivity until a peaceful world permits it to be indulged without
strain is to postpone it for ever. It is also, though this is a
long and complicated story, to weaken any possibility of
diminishing the irrationalities of the world. We have already
argued that all but a few people can tolerate but a very brief
sojourn in universities; most people prefer to spend their
lives improving the world rather than studying it. This is a
legitimate preference, but it is not a legitmate reason for
insisting that no other view is to be taken. Sophistries of this
kind were particularly prominent among American academics who during the 1960s became passionately committed
to opposition to the Vietnam involvement. Many such
humane and generous sentiments become sophistries if
pressed too far outside their proper context.

A similar judgement must be made of the view that
academic inquiry is fundamentally ideological because some
of its conclusions are used, or misused, by practical men.
When Kathleen Gough complains that anthropologists are
helping in the working of American counter-insurgency programmes and that this 'gives little reason to hope that the
field will soon salvage its autonomy as a humane endeavour'⁸
one can only comment that there is *nothing* in the world
which cannot be used for bad purposes, irrespective of what
we may regard as good or bad purposes. The notion that
the doctor, for example, also makes the most efficient
murderer appears in Plato's dialogues, though Plato himself
never developed this into the vulgar doctrine that nothing is
good or bad but using makes it so. This latter doctrine sometimes appears in attempts to foist upon scientists a special

⁷ Marvin Surkin, 'Sense and Non-Sense in Politics', in Marvin Surkin and Alan
Wolfe (eds), *An End to Political Science*, New York 1970.
⁸ Kathleen Gough, 'World Revolution and the Science of Man', in Theodore
Roszak (ed), *The Dissenting Academy*, London 1969, pp. 228–9.

responsibility for the uses to which their theories are put. But unless we regard a scientist's theory as a form of property limiting its use by other men, it should be clear that the skill of constructing scientific theories is not to be identified with the skill of wisely judging social and political consequences. In any case, the question of social consequences is a peculiarly difficult one. The interaction of events soon becomes impossibly complicated, and there is no point at which we may stop a snowball of consequences in order to declare a moral judgement upon it.

A related argument about universities – related because it must be put in the category of *cris de coeur* rather than of serious argument – is the view that intellectuals have a peculiar burden in the way of diffusing the truth. Noam Chomsky states this view as: 'It is the responsibility of intellectuals to speak the truth and to expose lies.'[9] A tolerably full understanding of the significance of this remark would require an examination of the ways in which intellectuals have tried to argue themselves into a special and priestly status in modern societies. Karl Mannheim's view that only intellectuals, being loosely attached to social structures, have a chance of freedom from the cognitively determining effects of 'total ideologies' is another example of the same attitude.[10] All that needs to be done in this context, however, is to say that it is the responsibility of *all* citizens to speak the truth, and that while intellectuals have certain talents in this endeavour, they also have special burdens. Spending so much of their lives among theories which can safely be hard and precise because they are held hypothetically, intellectuals are particularly prone to mistake a system, model or theory for what we may naively call 'reality itself'. This disposition sometimes renders them dogmatic, so that their cries become increasingly insistent at just the moment they are sinking helplessly into the ambiguities of the practical world.

[9] Noam Chomsky, 'The Responsibility of the Intellectuals' in Roszak, *op. cit.*, p. 142.
[10] Karl Mannheim, *Ideology and Utopia*, Bonn 1930.

168

Professor Chomsky illustrates this himself in his use of the word 'invasion' when he goes on to insist that 'the deceit and distortion surrounding the American invasion of Vietnam is by now so familiar that it has lost its power to shock'. The curious effect of schematic thinking when directly applied to the practical world is to generate melodrama – or ideology, which is the intellectual version of melodrama. Professor Chomsky's world shrinks to a conflict of courageous truth-telling intellectuals against deceitful politicians, aided by those academics (on the other side) whom the politicians have managed to corrupt.

We may conclude our discussion of rhetorical attacks upon the objectivity of academic inquiry by unravelling what is assumed in a typical demand for academic commitment to a political cause: 'Can one remain silent in the face of an immoral war and counter that he is not being political?'[11] The question takes it for granted that neutrality[12] is not a possible position in a political conflict, and when the doctrine is being formulated with an eye to profundity, it becomes: not to take up a position is itself a position. There is, of course, good biblical warrant for the doctrine. In relation to the Vietnam War, which happens to have been the circumstance eliciting many of these arguments, we may distinguish the three possible positions of support, opposition and neutrality. It is obvious that in terms of this simple schema, neutrals constitute a pool from whom both sides will try to recruit. The *political* issue is one of trying to stampede the neutrals into one corral or the other, and the doctrine we are considering is a practical device for doing so. But it is only plausible to collapse these three positions into an essential two if we confuse the issue with another quite different one: What is the practical effect of taking up

---

[11] Alan Wolfe, 'The Professional Mystique' in Surkin and Wolfe, *op. cit.*, p. 292.

[12] To be neutral is to take up a position in relation to some outside issue; from which it will be clear that on my view of academic inquiry a don's work is not neutral with regard to outside events but quite irrelevant to them. Neutrality is a virtue of good journalists, not academics. But this is a refinement that need not be considered in this context.

each of these positions? And the answer given by the dualists is that a neutral stance has the effect of helping those who are in favour of continuing the war. Whether this is actually so depends upon the details. For it is sometimes the case that, through ambiguous circumstances, those who are against a war have the practical effect of prolonging it. They may, for example, encourage longer a futile resistance. Or it may be that those who are in favour of a war serve to shorten it, because, being unsavoury people, their support has the effect of strengthening the opposition. Any number of things may happen in politics, and all that a philosophical analysis of this kind can achieve is to lay out the possibilities, especially the possibilities that may be ignored. What effect the 'neutrality' of academics has on practical situations depends entirely upon the details of those situations. We may, then, recognize this particular argument as a rhetorical sophistry designed to encourage people to take up ill-considered political opinions on questions for which they have no direct responsibility. We may, indeed, recognize it for something more : as an instance of the pervasive tendency of ideological thinking to reduce all complexities to the single standard of : which side of the struggle is this opinion on?[13]

We may now move to more sophisticated and genuinely philosophical arguments in favour of the view that universities systematically support something often imprecisely specified as the 'status quo'. The term has lost the benefit of italics in recent times because it has become so thoroughly domesticated. Let us take the view that to explain is inevitably to justify. Robin Blackburn argues that 'the prevailing ideology in the field of the social sciences as taught in British universities and colleges consistently defends the existing social arrangements of the capitalist world'. This is a bold universal of the type we have already discussed in the

---

[13] Herbert Marcuse may be taken to illustrate this ideological disposition: 'In the contemporary period, all historical projects tend to be polarised on the two conflicting totalities – capitalism and communism . . .' *One-Dimensional Man*, London 1964, ch. 9 *ad fin*.

case of Anthony Arblaster, and, as in that case, its boldness shrinks somewhat on examination. For what we next learn is that 'It endeavours to suppress the idea that any preferable alternative does or could exist.'[14] Now whether or not this is true, it is clear that academic inquiry as we have described it is not at all concerned with 'preferable alternatives'. Such matters belong to the practical world; and we may recognize this argument as a disguised form of plea for the bringing into academic inquiry of a set of practical issues. The same comment may be made of an American version of the same argument: 'That the dominant academic ideology, commonly identified as "pluralism", cannot diagnose the problems and cannot offer an adequate strategy for change has been persuasively argued in many places'[15] Here again, the demand is for practical involvement; and in both cases the existence of a 'dominant academic ideology' is merely taken for granted.

A much more sophisticated argument of this form is presented by Alasdair MacIntyre. His particular target is a hypothesis advanced in the 1950s by such sociologists as Edward Shils, Daniel Bell and Seymour Martin Lipset that passionate ideological commitment was giving way to consensual politics as a direct response to the changing structure of modern industrial societies. Professor MacIntyre argues that the 'end of ideology' thesis was itself a piece of ideology actually promoting what it purported to describe.[16] For, so the argument runs, such a description tends to be taken by those who read it rather as a norm to be obeyed. Now as to the practical effect of academic theories, nothing regular may be said. Sociology counts among its more entertaining bits of folklore a set of somewhat lunatic people who seem to have read the Kinsey Report on sexual behaviour as instruction about how people of such and such an age or class *ought* to behave. No doubt there are such people, but there are also

[14] Robin Blackburn, 'A Brief Guide to Bourgeois Ideology' in Alexander Cockburn and Robin Blackburn (eds), *Student Power*, London 1961, p. 163.
[15] David Kettler, 'Beyond Republicanism: The Socialist Critique of Political Idealism', in Surkin and Wolfe, *op. cit.*, p. 34.
[16] Alasdair MacIntyre, *Against the Self Images of the Age*, London 1971, p. 3.

other people whose response is exactly the opposite. And it would seem that this kind of contingent social perversity is exactly what happened to the 'end of ideology' thesis; for the consensual decade of the 1950s was followed in America by the violently ideological decade of the 1960s. Some sort of involvement of the theories of the social sciences with the actual behaviour of human beings is perhaps unavoidable. It is one of the many well-known burdens a social scientist has to carry. But it is clear that the career of the 'end of ideology' thesis is that it was advanced as an academic hypothesis, proved to be wrong in certain respects, and has been modified or abandoned. Such is the normal destiny of academic theories. But no one shouted it as a slogan; nor did it feature upon the banners carried by masses. Professor MacIntyre himself is, in the same article, clear enough about what an ideology is. One of the features he notes is that an ideology 'is not merely believed by the members of a given social group, but believed in such a way that it at least partially defines for them their social existence'.[17] This is a very plausible view; and it refutes MacIntyre's own argument; for it would be absurd to suggest that Bell, Shils, and Lipset had their social existence defined for them by the doctrine they advanced.

In spite of these defects, this line of attack would, if cogently developed, suggest an important criticism of the way in which the social sciences are taught in universities. If one approaches the study of a modern society with the presumption that the task is to produce a scientific explanation, then one has to assume that everything that one studies is part of some 'system'. For in scientific terms, explanation tends to consist of exhibiting what is to be explained as part of a system. This is why scientific explanation may be plausibly construed in the mechanistic terms of cause and effect. Modern life, in these terms, must appear as an interlocking complex of functions, in which policemen and criminals,

[17] *Ibid.*, p. 6. Cf. also Lipset's claim that his views had been misrepresented, *Encounter*, Dec. 1972.

172

voters and politicians, clergymen and sinners, apologists and critics are all part of a mechanical system. This system *could not be other than it is*, for if it were, then the phenomena would not have been explained in the required terms. The behavioural study of social and political life therefore deliberately limits itself to externals: to the instances of things happening, and to correlations between them. There is no place in this model of explanation for agony, doubt, the consideration of alternatives: no room, that is, for all the *deliberative* phenomena which cannot be registered in terms of empirical investigation. Even the attempt to study deliberation in these terms necessarily turns it into something systematic: it becomes decision-theory.

Now those who mistake the methodological assumptions of any science for a description of how they themselves behave are likely to share the feelings of the celebrated:

> Young man who said 'Damn!
> To think that I am what I am;
> A creature that moves in predestinate grooves;
> Not even a bus, but a tram.'

That young man is now out on the streets chalking 'smash the system' on every open space he finds. And he is perfectly right in feeling that there is something wrong with this picture of human life. He is merely foolish in making the intellectual's mistake of thinking that what he has been taught is actually reality. Such people are, of course, also misguided in thinking that they can 'smash the system', for even their ambition to smash it will very soon appear as one more feature of the system itself. As indeed it is, so long as we take a behavioural view of what is involved in studying human life. There are, of course, alternative historical and philosophical ways of understanding human behaviour, and they too are cultivated in universities. They all have their limits, and academic life is in part constituted by a continuing discussion of this very question. What cannot be

173

done is to dismiss these discussions as merely reflections of some deeper social forces.

Much the most famous and most direct attack upon the intellectual autonomy of universities takes the form of asserting that their attempts at evaluative neutrality are doomed by the very logic of inquiry. This is very commonly stated as one more of the bold universals with which this field is thickly populated. Seriously thought out arguments for it, however, are relatively rare. Thus we are told by Kathleen Gough[18] that values 'do enter anthropological research at many points, whether this is recognized or not. They enter into the selection of problems, the choice of variables, and thus the interpretation of data'. This is a plausible enough position, since everything that we do is, in one important sense at least, practical. It involves the practical judgement that whatever we do is worth doing in preference to some possible alternative. But this is an exiguous little point unless it is used to reveal to us the great mass of fascinating and worthwhile subjects which we might equally well be exploring were we not tethered to the values we espouse. But the horse of criticism generally shies at this, the crucial, fence. What Miss Gough supplies us with is a further general statement: 'The "ethical neutrality" position seems to be taken up as an excuse for not espousing unpopular viewpoints or getting into controversies.' We are now in a position to recognize this charge of cowardice as our old friend, the complaint that academics are not involving themselves in good causes. And this impression is hardly to be altered by considering the only concrete suggestion actually made: 'Anthropologists have failed to evaluate and analyse, as a world social system and an interconnected political economy, the structure of Western imperialism and the common and variant features of its impact on the non-Western world.'[19] Since the concept of imperialism, as developed by Hobson and Lenin, is essentially a political concept which has been used for a great

18 Kathleen Gough, *op. cit.*, p. 136.
19 *Ibid.*, p. 135,

number of political purposes and has consequently developed all the rich ambiguity of practice, this suggestion amounts to the familiar demand that academic disciplines should set themselves up as research departments of some ideological proposition. No academic is likely to take very seriously the notion that the entire texture of world events in the twentieth century constitutes a single 'system' having regular features and a single analysable mode of operation. It might be possible to develop, as a serious academic hypothesis, something like this belief, though such a theory would be subject to the objections we have just outlined to any subsumption of human behaviour under a comprehensive 'system'. But outside this possibility, the notion of imperialism is no more than a popular political belief lacking in explanatory force.

The same kind of argument commonly appears in discussions of economics. Robin Blackburn remarks that 'the very concept of "exploitation" is anathema since it questions the assumed underlying harmony of interests within a capitalist society'.[20] This suggestion is followed by another use of the bold universal: 'By excluding *a priori* such ways of analysing economic relationships, modern bourgeois economics ensures that discussion will never be able to question the capitalist property system.' This largely depends upon a misunderstanding of economics, whose concepts are concerned, to use the time-hallowed formula, with the consequences of choosing between scarce resources, and there are hardly any of its concepts (including profit) which are not equally applicable to a socialist or a capitalist economy. The concept of 'exploitation' is indeed not taken seriously by economists, for it is essentially evaluative. Economic abstractions are defined in terms of each other so as to compose a model whose test is how effectively it explains actual economic quantities. The concept of 'exploitation' is a political and moral term based upon moral elements which have no place in economic theory. On the other hand, there is nothing at all in economic science which

20 Robin Blackburn, in Blackburn and Cockburn, *op. cit.*, p. 166.

prohibits anyone from saying that such and such a set of workers are being exploited, even though they may be getting the market wage. Hence Blackburn's view that economic science is constructed so as to 'ensure that discussion will never be able to question the capitalist property system' is not only false in fact (because the woods are full of such doubters, himself included) but confused in logic. The same considerations apply when this view is projected back into history: 'Adam Smith valued liberty,' writes Sumner Rosen,[21] 'Ricardo productivity and progress, Marx the elimination of exploitation, Keynes the achievement of full employment. These provided the normative tests by which they judged the economic systems about which they wrote (or dreamed), and on them they built their recommended solutions. Even when writing abstractly, economists imply, presuppose, a system and a set of values by which they judge and invite judgement. The economic ideologies derive from these roots.' It is true, indeed, that Keynes (for example) valued full employment, but it is untrue that this makes him a great economist. For what Keynes supplied was a new theory of the inter-relationships of economic variables (including, also, a few new variables), and his economic significance stands or falls on the fruitfulness of this new theory. The theory, indeed, is just as convenient a device for *preventing* full employment as it is for facilitating it. Rosen's general argument seems to be in the same case as most of the assaults upon academic autonomy already cited: the promise of these bold assertions far exceeds the performance of the evidence cited. 'The stress on scientism', he writes, seeming to mean by 'scientism' the concern to avoid taking up moral stances, 'is itself a kind of ideology; it suggests that the central values of the economic tradition in the West – free markets, efficiency, growth – are sufficiently valid for our time to require no further serious scrutiny.' And all one can say to this, rather wearisome, reiteration is that the desire to study economic phenomena scientifically suggests nothing of the

[21] 'Keynes Without Gadflies', in Roszak, *op. cit.*, p. 83.

sort, and that there are, as a simple matter of fact, plenty of economists who do not regard free markets, efficiency, and growth as desirable. What, one can only wonder, have these critics been reading? And since they are mostly themselves academics, do they not refute themselves?

Nor is the case much better if one moves into the cloudier realms of Herbert Marcuse, who is currently the most celebrated exponent of this view. Since Marcuse virtually never uses a genuine concrete example of what he is saying, it is difficult to be specific in refuting him. What seems to be the key passion in his thought on this subject is a desire to penetrate beyond the surface of things as they appear in Western societies to a hidden dimension which turns out to be the political realities of an ideologist:

Under the repressive conditions in which men think and live, thought—any mode of thinking which is not confined to pragmatic orientation within the status quo—can recognize the facts and respond to the facts only by 'going behind' them. Experience takes place before a curtain which conceals and, if the world is the appearance of something behind the curtain of immediate experience, then, in Hegel's terms, it is we ourselves who are behind the curtain.[22]

One-Dimensional Man spends his life behind this curtain. But that the curtain (evidently an iron curtain) is a property of politics seems clear when we observe the tinge of melodrama which Marcuse can give to the simplest things:

Analytic philosophy often spreads the atmosphere of denunciation and investigation by committee. The intellectual is called on the carpet. What do you mean when you say...? Don't you conceal something? You talk a language which is suspect.... You don't talk like the rest of us, like the man in the street, but rather like a foreigner who does not belong here. We have to cut you down to size, expose your tricks, purge you. We shall teach you to say what you have in mind, to 'come clean', 'to put your cards on the table'...[23]

[22] *One-Dimensional Man*, p. 149.
[23] *Ibid., op. cit.*, p. 154.

177

And so on, in the same vein, As an account of linguistic philosophy, this seems to be so completely false as to be only explicable in terms of Marcuse's personal biography as a German refugee living in America. It is certainly not at all a serious criticism of linguistic philosophy. Marcuse appears as a man who, however far he may roam through the fields of abstraction, remains tethered to the fundamental ideological reality of The Struggle. The key reality of the twentieth century is the concentration camp, and whatever does not express that reality is presented as an illicit obscuring of reality.

Similar considerations apply to pupils of Marcuse, such as Jurgen Habermas, who attempt to argue the same case. In an article dedicated to Marcuse, Habermas, has argued that 'rationality' in science is a form of bourgeois ideology:

The progressive 'rationalization' of society is linked to the institutionalization of scientific and technical development. To the extent that technology and science permeate social institutions and thus transform them, old legitimations are destroyed. The secularization and 'disenchantment' of action-orienting world-views, of cultural tradition as a whole, is the obverse of the growing 'rationality' of social action. . . . Marcuse is convinced that what Weber called 'rationalization' realizes not rationality as such but rather, in the name of rationality, a specific form of unacknowledged political domination. . . . By virtue of its structure, purposive-rational action is the exercise of control.[24]

It would seem, though it would take a bold reader to be entirely confident, that Marcuse and Habermas are concerned with the fact that Western technology (though not Western science) has emerged out of a doctrine, deriving from theology, about man's divine mission to exploit nature. Both can see the possibility of an alternative view of nature: 'We can seek out a fraternal rather than an exploited nature. At the level of an as yet incomplete intersubjectivity we can impute subjectivity to animals and plants, even to minerals, and try to communicate with nature instead of merely proces-

[24] Jurgen Habermas, *Towards a Rational Society*, London 1971, pp. 81–2.

sing her under conditions of severed communication.'[25] While there are some eccentric features of this view, it will not seem entirely dotty in view of the fears of world pollution which became current in the early 1970s. Even Bertrand Russell, just before his death, was beginning to advocate a kind of secular piety towards nature. What is objectionable about the Marcuse-Habermas argument however is the attempt to push these values presumed to underlie Western technology one further stage up the level of abstraction so that they may be inserted in the logical structure of rationality itself. The fundamental weapon used by ideologists attempting to deny the autonomy of academic inquiry is the insertion of matters of substance into categories of logic, so that nothing is left untouched by the ideologist's primary concern: ideology itself.

It would merely be tedious to continue exemplifying this line of thought. Tedious, and also irrelevant to what is really involved. For what generates these arguments is very seldom a theory of academic inquiry; it is, rather, a response to the excitement of an ideological commitment. For we are dealing above all with an area of thought which excites people profoundly. For the most part, men are prepared to kill each other only for political or religious reasons, and it is politics and religion which are, in conversation, likely to provoke people into irrational and intemperate affirmation or denial. Part of the explanation of the strength of ideology must be sought in the effects of transferred excitement. The general principle which applies here is that whatever is thought to explain an exciting subject will itself be found exciting. Under ordinary conditions, economics, sociology, psychology or biology are no more and no less exciting than any other academic field of inquiry. But if an ideologist appears who purports to explain religious or political matters in terms of any one of them, then the excitement is transferred from the *explanandum* to the *explanans*. For this reason, the ideologically committed man brings to the study of whatever

[25] *Ibid.*, p. 88.

179

subject is relevant (economics or history to a Marxist, biology and anthropology to a racialist, etc) a quality of excitement and a degree of intensity which will not be found among its more orthodox practitioners. But this also makes the ideologist an irritable and fidgety colleague. He has no patience with many academic questions because he already knows the meaning of his subject matter. *His* economics are there to condemn the capitalist system. *His* psychology exhibits the mechanics of religion as an illusion. *His* sociology reveals the class secrets of politics which ordinary political rhetoric tries to conceal. *His* ethnology demonstrates the relative values of different races. And yet, many of his academic colleagues remain resistant to this meaning. This cannot be a genuine disagreement, for the ideologist is aware both of the truth of his own position, and also of the tendency of men to believe whatever is convenient and comfortable to them. Consequently, he concludes that they have been 'conditioned' by the system within which they live. There is, in ideological attitudes, much to support the truism that we tend to think of ourselves as free and of others as determined.

This connection between ideological commitment and academic self-esteem is sometimes supported by a fallacious identification. Universities are critical institutions; and each ideologist is aware of being 'critical of the society we live in'. The conclusion sometimes seems to follow that a university is only critical if it takes up towards the world the same attitude as the ideologist. It only *seems* to follow, however, by committing the fallacy known as undistributed middle. For the point is that ideologists, like any believers, are 'critical' in the sense that they reject the arguments of other people. The flat-earth society is an intensely critical body, and astrologers don't have much good to say about those irrationalists who believe in chance or accident. *Everybody* is, in this sense, critical, for this kind of criticism is merely the self-defence of believers. It is invariably accompanied by a pious and unquestioning addiction to the tenets of the belief held. Academic criticism is another kind of thing altogether, in both its quality and range. The argument depends, therefore, upon an equivocation in the meaning of 'criticism' and rests upon an undistributed middle term.

The arguments reviewed in this chapter may all be understood as responses to a disappointment. Both ideological thinking and journalism deal in such exciting subjects as wars and revolutions. Both types of attention to the world play upon human passions like admiration and contempt, compassion and envy. Both, in other words, encourage passionate commitment. They are, in the terms we have been using, essentially practical. And they encourage people to come up to universities in order to find out the 'real causes' of exciting things. But a large part of this excitement, being moral judgement, stands as a barrier to academic understanding. It is only by abandoning moral and emotional judgements, and attempting to see things cool, that we may begin to understand them academically. And this is something for which many people have little taste. Most people most of the time are concerned to understand things only so much as is necessary to improve them. The academic can only understand them better if he leaves improvement in other hands. Thus the dilemma which we noted in discussing the academic and the practical worlds reappears here as part of the explanation of why so many people find universities very disappointing places.

It remains, however, to consider one final and possibly fatal objection to the argument of this section. For if what we have been arguing is itself academic, and if it is destructive of some ideological beliefs, does it not follow that academic criticism has lost its remoteness and taken a particular side? Part of the answer to this objection is that academic criticism, like rain and the judgement of God, falls impartially upon all ideologies. A further part of the answer lies in an understanding of ideologies as attempts to smuggle moral and political policies into material presented as entirely academic. In such material, policies are like small children who imagine that they disappear if they merely close their eyes. But to destroy this pretence is not to destroy the policies; it merely opens the eyes. To say that the ideological reasons for promoting such and such a policy (making a revolution, to take a current example) are bad reasons is not at all to argue against the policy; still less is it to advocate an alternative. For any policy may be supported by bad reasons, and the world cannot be made safe for bad reasons. Furthermore, although it may be the case that a supporter of a policy whose reasons have thus been knocked away will abandon the policy, it is much more likely that he will think up better reasons. No doubt the reasons for a policy have some effect upon its nature, and in that sense academic criticism may directly affect the world. A neutral, it should be remembered, is a non-combatant: this does not mean that neutrals do not affect the world they live in, but they affect it in varied and complicated ways.

Part Three
The Siege of Academe

9 The Doctrine of Social Adaptation

We have so far identified a university as the location of a very specific kind of understanding of the world, and we have taken pains to distinguish this understanding from journalism and other forms of practical intellectuality. We must now consider it as an identity under constant siege from those who would take it over and bend it to their purposes. Universities have from early times been flattered, bribed, bullied and cajoled into serving one or other of the political and religious movements which have prospered in modern times. We generally imagine attacks on the university in terms of Nazi or Communist totalitarianism. For depth, these images are commonly stiffened by reference to a now dim legend of the Inquisition, and by more recent references to the complex events subsumed in the United States under the name of McCarthyism. But the very obviousness of such brutal attacks upon academic autonomy renders them, for our purposes, intellectually uninteresting. No one is likely to think that book-burning or loyalty oaths have much to do with academic inquiry. But pages of mellifluous (and generally tedious) prose about the purpose of the University and its relation to Society will be less easily recognized as an attempt to make the university an instrument of some social cause. Our concern in this section will be with a set of

185

formulae which appear whenever the attempt to create academic subservience is under way.

Since we are determined to avoid the danger of setting fire to straw men, let us take two brief examples of the kind of elevated rhetoric by which academics are sometimes seduced:

The university will be able to make its contribution to a free society only to the extent that it overcomes the temptation to conform unthinkingly to the prevailing ideology and to the existing patterns of power and privilege. In its relation to society, a free university should be expected to be, in a sense, 'subversive'. We take for granted that creative work in any field will challenge prevailing orthodoxy . . .

And again:

In the past, however, it was usually only the rich who could send their sons to university to fit them for playing a full role in society, rather than for acquiring a narrowly academic training. Now a minority privilege is becoming the need of the majority. This means that universities will have to provide a different and broader kind of education than much that is now given: with the emphasis on turning out useful citizens who can adapt to our complex, changing society, rather than specialized scholars.[1]

The key term in both passages is 'Society' (generally deserving to be capitalized), and in both cases universities are seen as contributory parts of this larger whole. 'Society' is a word which gets its plausibility from purporting to include everything we do, and its usefulness from its curious capacity to tell us what we ought to do. It is, then, a paradoxical term. It refers to the total context in which we live, and thereby acquires many of the same religious overtones which in Christian discourse attached to 'the World'.[2] And just as

[1] The first passage is by Noam Chomsky, and is taken from 'The Function of the University in a Time of Crisis', in *The Great Ideas Today, 1969*, Chicago, p. 45; the second from an editorial in the *Observer* for 15 December 1963. Both passages are of interest purely for their typicality.

[2] The resonance of the term 'society' in the second half of the twentieth century is one of the main clues to some of the period's deeper currents. But it will be obvious that, for our argument, the point is that 'society' stands essentially for what we

the world (or the creation) was ambiguous in Christian terms (being both God's workmanship and also an arena of temptations), so the current use of 'Society' may be found in two versions illustrated in the above quotations. In one version, Society stands for something to be resisted ('patterns of power and privileges'), and in the other version, it represents the totality of man's advancing endeavours, and therefore something to which we ought to attune ourselves. In both cases, a moral and religious prescription has been transposed into a sociological vocabulary. It is this face alone which makes it inappropriate to detect clichés in the passages we have quoted; for they have rather the character of a litany. Unless we recognize this feature of such discourse, we should have to dismiss the words of Noam Chomsky, for example, as self-refuting, since they are themselves the statement of 'a prevailing orthodoxy'.

Menenius Agrippa, explaining in *Coriolanus* to the plebs of Rome that they were mutinous members against the all-sustaining belly, was no more traditional in his addiction to the organic view of society than these educational rhetoricians who would extinguish academic independence by a functional exhortation to adapt to the larger whole. The larger whole may be called 'society' or it may be called 'a free society', but it is generally given an uplifting label, and it is commonly seen as in the process of change. The doctrine of social adaptation points to presumed changes in 'Society' and argues the necessity of corresponding changes in the contributory part: i.e., in the university. The language of social functions and social purposes (which we discussed in the Introduction) lends intellectual elevation to what is basically a form of moral coercion. Abstractly stated, the doctrine is immediately and clearly refutable. For it assumes that the thing referred to as 'Society' is a coherent system of

have called 'the practical world' and that *any* attempt to understand the University in terms of it begins by begging the main question. I have dealt with some of the issues raised by this troublesome and elusive concept in *The Liberal Mind*, London, 1963, chapter 5.

functions. But if this assumption is correct, then universities do in fact perform what is required of them, and no adjustment is necessary; and if universities are not actually performing the function, then the assumption that Society is a system must be discarded as false. The notion of Society as a system of functions turns out to be, not an account of social life, but a propagandist device for imposing changes upon it.

But like most decisive philosophical refutations, this argument runs the risk of missing the point. For the practical question raised by the argument results from the attempt to rationalize activities. People and institutions alike tend to fall into habits derived from situations which have long ceased to exist; and we may save ourselves from such pointless repetition if we seek out and judge the reasons for our actions. We may try to test social institutions in a similar way. To ask, for example, the purpose of an army is likely to elicit the reply that armies are for defence, which implies that any army which becomes excessively pre-occupied with parade-ground finesse, the making of *coups d'états,* or interfactional rivalries is not fulfilling its purposes; similarly an addiction to bows and arrows at a time when gunpowder had become the rule would no doubt indicate a hazardous failure of adaptation.

In everyday life, this utilitarian attitude to many things we do is both common and necessary. But even in everyday life we recognize that this attitude can become a mania, and that a man who, lying idly in a deckchair on a sunny Sunday afternoon, is troubled by the question: What is the purpose of my leisure? must be counted as inserting the wrong key in the lock of understanding. This is a case where the very question: What is the point? shows that the point has already been missed. It *is* possible to construe marriages in terms of procreation, friendships in terms of some human need for companionship, philosophy in terms of man's need to understand his environment, and play in terms of a discharge of tensions: possible, but also vacuous. For these are spontaneous human acts, subserving no supposedly superior

purposes, and they may be described, just as academic inquiry is often described, as 'disinterested'. They are 'disinterested' not in the sense that they do not serve any interest
or have any purpose, but that they are not related to this purpose or interest as a means to an end. They are undertaken
for the sake of engaging in them, not for achieving anything
extrinsic to them.

On these grounds, we may recognize questions like : What
is the purpose of a university? or: What duties does a
university owe to society? as fundamentally illicit, irrespective of any answers that may be made to them. It is true, of
course, that universities both affect and are affected by their
social circumstances. From society they get the resources to
maintain themselves, and to society they supply educated
men capable of skill and innovation, refuges for the
scholarly, an occupation for some of the young, a store of
memory, and so on. It is when these complicated inter-
relationships are described in the functional terms of a social
system that a slant is being placed upon the facts which the
evidence will not sustain. It does not matter whether the
supposed function is 'to challenge the prevailing orthodoxies', 'to facilitate national development', 'to maintain the
purity of faith and morals' or 'to act as the intellectual power-
house of society'. There are dozens of such formulae, and
although some of them point to perfectly real effects of
academic inquiry, none of them can claim any serious normative status. Nor does it matter whether these suggested
functions are advanced as values to be embraced or follies to
be abandoned. Thus the view that universities have, in the
past, produced a 'privileged elite' and that they ought to be
open to the whole of society is both historically nonsensical
and philosophically uncomprehending. For all views that the
university either does or ought to serve 'society', that it ought
to be the instrument of something external to the academic
world, are devices for denying academic independence, and
for imposing alien values upon it.

Further, the very use of the word 'Society' serves merely to obfuscate the character of those alien values. When Professor Raymond Williams writes 'I agree, in principle, that a society has a right to make demands on its educational system ...'[3] he is fashionably taking 'Society' to be a coherent whole of which it makes sense to say that 'it' has demands, and which ought to be served by its parts (such as universities). But as a simple matter of fact, 'Society' (being simply the agglomeration of social activities) is not the sort of entity that can possibly 'make demands' upon anything. Specific people (or the governing bodies of institutions, including the State itself) can indeed make demands, but to talk of 'Society' doing so is nonsensical. It merely serves the propagandist purpose of dressing some of those demands in borrowed grandeur.[4]

Anyone faced with so crude a piece of intellectual coercion will be tempted to reverse the critical question. Instead of asking : Why ought universities to serve Society? a critic will be tempted to inquire : Why ought not Society to serve the universities? During the Middle Ages it did precisely that, largely because of the religious associations of academic corporations. But in modern times there is an obvious riposte to our reversed question. It is that Society (in effect, the state as a taxing agency) supplies most of the money for academic institutions, and need not support institutions which contribute nothing to it.

To deal adequately with this view requires us to recognize

[3] 'The Teaching Relationship: Both Sides of the Wall', in Rubinstein and Stoneman, *op. cit.*, p. 207.

[4] The requirements of due proportion forbid us to go into the mechanics of this style of propaganda; but they do not forbid us observing that the popularity of 'Society' in this role is probably connected with the happy inventiveness it allows to pundits to pass off their own sentiments as being widely, even universally, entertained, rather as a ventriloquial dummy is the mouthpiece of the ventriloquist. Thus, when Professor Williams goes on to remark: 'But if there is discontent among the students, there is also discontent among the teachers, since we are all victims of the same system, and even those who play along with it usually have, in private, few illusions about what is really happening', we can only wonder at his supernatural percipience, and at the confidence with which he attributes to everyone such confident knowledge of 'what is really happening'.

that we are in an area of conflicting desirabilities. It is today commonly thought desirable that everyone both capable of and eager for a university education should have one. But in practice this desirability brings with it an undesirable increase in the state control of education. If state control increases, universities will have been forced into submission, and they will cease to be what they were. The consequence would seem to be that the granting of a universal right to enter the academic world appears to involve the extinction of the right, since the promised education will have changed its character. What we have to deal with is the common political situation where a desirability (such as the extension of university education) and an undesirability (such as the increase of state power) are yoked together, and the one involves the other. A conceivable solution of the problem would be for the state to provide the money, and yet refrain from exercising the control; and indeed, from the institution of the University Grants Committee in Britain until recent times (a period of half a century dating from 1919), this is virtually what happened. But such a degree of government self-abnegation requires unusual qualities in a civil society; it is like asking the lion to lie down with the lamb – something possible only until the lion develops an appetite. Once the sums of money spent on education become so large as to encroach very seriously upon alternative governmental spending, governments seek control. There are often good reasons why they do so; and some of their demands are not unwise: it is not so much wisdom as independence which is at issue. Further, some people may be found to welcome the entry of governments into education, for they dream dreams of an ideal model of education, and entertain hopes that they may be able to influence the government to create it. Educational thought has long been abuzzing with the ideas of people infatuated with some universal system, and for whom the advocacy of rights to education would seem to be no more than an oblique way of getting governments involved in educational policy. And the fact that this is a bitter pill is recognized in the abundance of rhetorical sugaring, in the form of promises of or demands for greater democracy or greater participation.

There is, in abstract terms, a paradoxical element in governmental control of universities: for what the government controls is unlikely to be a university. But this formal relationship needs to be qualified by the recognition that the academic world is one thing and institutional arrangements another. Just as churches have been known to thrive on persecution, so the academic world may remain alive and vital under unpropitious institutional circumstances, while it may wither and die as the result of self-seeking or political commitment among institutionally unconstrained dons. In spite of this, the formal relationship also describes a tendency in the real world, and no one who cares for the academic world will be wise to encourage the political control of universities. Equally, governments who care for the vitality of civilization will prefer to allow autonomy to universities.

The doctrine of social adaptation may operate with some such holistic concept as 'Society', but is likely in doing so to fall into absurdities. Thus grandiose remarks about education 'reflecting social values' can only invite us to wonder what social values could possibly be involved in construing Virgil, or in following a proof of the Pythagorean theory. Some of these problems may be avoided if the doctrine switches from something cloudy and vacuous (such as 'Society') to something rather more specific. The idea of a 'system of education', for example, can be used to impose a rather different kind of contributory role on universities, without requiring a writer to abandon the assumption that 'Society' is a single coherent entity which speaks with a single voice. Nor does it matter, for most purposes, whether the transposition assumes that there *does* exist such a thing as a 'system of education' (and that it is bad) or that no such thing exists (but that it must be created). To assume that there is such a thing as a system of education in such

192

countries as Britain and America is obviously the less plausible view to take. For it is clear from the history of education that the schools and universities of Britain, for example, grew up over a long period of time and as a result of a very miscellaneous set of impulses. It is only since 1870 that the government has taken any very serious interest in education; and the manner of that interest was for a long time merely one of supplementation and of maintenance of standards. As late as 1963, the Robbins Report was perfectly clear that no such thing as a 'system' of education existed in Great Britain. This has not prevented the expression 'victims of the system' being applied both to teachers and pupils. But such an expression reveals a religious view of things which will be discussed in the next chapter; it is largely confined to people who seem incapable of disapproving of anything unless it has first been understood as a 'system'.

More commonly, the doctrine appears in a form which takes the existence of a system for granted and makes recommendations about how the system should change. Thus when we encounter the doctrine that university education has been regarded as 'a privilege for a small elite' and that we should 'think more in terms of producing a broad upper echelon of intelligence – qualified men and women trained in skills appropriate to post-war society',[5] we find the universities being construed not in terms of scholarship and understanding (which we have argued to constitute the core of academic identity) but as a productive system whose business it is to be attuned to social needs. This is the tune sung by modernizers interested in national efficiency, and these particular remarks were made in a context of national anxiety about technological competence. Hence, the skills which were then thought 'appropriate to post-war society' would not be the same as those thought desirable a decade earlier, and emphatically not those widely thought desirable even five years later. The effect of such proposals is abandonment of the academic world in favour of a constantly

[5] Noel Annan, 'The Universities', *Encounter*, April 1963, pp. 3, 13.

changing set of practical desirabilities. But the worst aspect of this line of thought is that, being concerned with a 'national' system of education, it not only makes schools dependent upon passing fashions, but also endeavours to make sure that no one shall escape this submission to the parochiality of the present moment. For addiction to national systems of education is almost invariably coupled with a powerful hostility to 'privilege', which must therefore be interpreted to the demagogic specification of anything that escapes the system.

It is also strange that advocacy of a national system of education should be currently widespread among people who otherwise pride themselves upon their attachment to liberty. The ancestors of such people in the nineteenth century experienced profound misgivings even at proposals for a limited intrusion of government into education. Their misgivings were based upon the assumption that education was a private matter (as it previously always had been), and that if it passed to the state it would constitute a dangerous reinforcement of the state's capacity for despotism. This belief was supported by the observation that both Napoleons, along with all the absolute monarchs of the continent, had always been enthusiastic supporters of a national system of education, and did not hesitate to use it for their own military and dynastic purposes. The first Napoleon had indeed inherited a national system of education from the centralizing governments of the French Revolution. The attitude of British liberals had been slowly modified, partly by the discretion of British governments, and partly by a recognition that the alternative to compulsory education was a large class of illiterates who would find themselves helpless in modern conditions. Nevertheless, they continued to find it important that British education should retain many centres of initiative, rather than that all initiative should be concentrated in the state: and such would be the situation if a national system of education were to be established.

Once this element of central direction has appeared,

education is removed from its fruitful obscurity and has to make its way in the glare of political limelight. Only when such a situation has been deliberately created (and it can come about no other way) does it even begin to make sense to say: 'The interrelations of a society and its educational system make it necessary to reform both together: the reform of education is part of a wider battle.'[6] Education, as a cultivation of the mind, having its own tradition which is in some degree independent of 'society', loses this character and becomes yoked to the fancied and fleeting utilities dreamed up by publicists and politicians. Although our concern is merely to emphasize that this is to stretch education on a rack, it is not entirely irrelevant to emphasize that it is also disastrous for other social activities. Where everything has become politics, then politics is left as the only vital thing in the state. The final outcome of a fully national system of education is a totalitarian society, where students are directed to study the skills the state currently imagines it will require, and where all the talk about change and adaptation cannot conceal the fundamentally static and unimaginative character of what is going on. For it is only thoroughly plural societies which have learned the secret of originality and development. A national system of education is therefore a recipe for decadence.

The doctrine of social adaptation results from taking as a description of the world a set of arguments developed as a rhetorical resource for advocating any set of proposed changes whatever, irrespective of their specific virtues. Just as anyone with a proposal to make, in council chamber, parliament and pub, may easily equip himself with a body of general reasons why change is difficult and fruitless, so these arguments may be countered by others (which are equally plausible) advocating change as a necessary part of our response to the conditions of life. The one set of arguments is commonly thought of as conservative, the other as radical.

[6] Rubinstein and Stoneman, *op. cit.*, Introduction, p. 23.

The doctrine of social adaptation is one of these general rhetorics, serving to bring to our attention those many features of life where things have changed recently, and to relegate to the back of our minds those respects in which human life remains much the same from generation to generation. There can be no doubt that the theory of evolution has sunk deep roots in the imaginations of Western people, and that many of them have developed an anxiety bordering upon hysteria not to embrace the fate of the scaly mastodon and the sabre-tooth tiger. Such people are eager to embrace novelties.

In the case of the universities, the doctrine of social adaptation carries with it not merely these curious echoes of Victorian beliefs about progress, but also a heavy charge of nationalist passion. The expansion of technological education in the United States in the 1960s depended upon competitive emulation of the Russian Sputnik. The foundation of six new universities in Britain about the same time resulted partly from a heavy deposit of unreliable statistics about the relative proportions of qualified manpower being trained by the major countries of the world. The idea was floated that economic growth (an ideal which long bewitched men's minds, only to be exorcized by the pollution scare) depended directly upon the number of educated people in a population. Like most delusions, this one is difficult to experience in retrospect: only the historian, tramping around among forgotten words and records, can experience the wonder occasioned by a direct confrontation with an old, abandoned folly. This particular folly was held with such fervour among the British of the time that some university students began to adopt the superior reighteous-ness which comes from imagining oneself a hot national resource. Those days have fortunately passed, but what has not passed is the disposition of the articulate public to keep a nervous eye on what is being done elsewhere.

Identical political calculations have been part of European

thinking over many centuries. Ivan the Terrible attempted to recruit technological experts to teach his backward subjects some of the mysteries of Western technical skill. He was frustrated by the town council of Lübeck, which imposed its own sixteenth-century version of a strategic arms embargo. Venice had great difficulty in preserving the secrets of its glass monopoly, in a world of realms jockeying for pre-eminence. In more recent times, the prestige of Germany after the Franco-Prussian war led most European states into programmes of social services and instructional expansion. Compulsory education for children in England dates from this period, and owed much to this stimulus. Nor need it be denied that skill and efficiency are national assets. Military capability over the last two centuries has been almost exactly correlated with industrial efficiency. The real mistake is to drag universities into this murky arena of political calculations as if they were nothing else but cogs in the system of instruction provided by the state.[7]

The general mistake involved in these cases is one of identifying universities in terms of their incidental benefits. It is as if a Beethoven string quartet were identified as a lullaby because it happened to put this or that child to sleep. The source of this very widespread fallacy lies in critics who have pushed analogies too far. Students at universities come up to examinations and pass out into the world almost as if universities were factories and graduates were its products. Again, students may choose from a great variety of courses and degrees, as if they had come to a cultural supermarket. Both analogies encourage the suggestion that universities

[7] It would fall outside the scope of this essay to consider all features of British education; but this is the place to note the suggestion that the coexistence of universities along with polytechnics and other forms of tertiary education in Britain constitutes an affront known with all the bogus technical chic of modern propaganda as 'the binary system'. Universities, so this expression is designed to suggest, are the spoilt children of advanced education when compared with polytechnics and teachers' training colleges. The solution suggested is not, it hardly needs to be said, to increase the independence of non-academic institutions, but rather to diminish the independence of universities by removing what are inevitably known as their 'privileges'.

197

should adapt themselves to changing demand. Yet even within the scope of analogies of this kind, experience suggests that the effect of market forces or of political opinion (the two sources of demands for change) has often been to destroy valuable craft work and to cheapen commodities for an undiscriminating mass market. The virtues of adaptation obviously depend on what is being adapted to, and an injudicious responsiveness has in the past constituted a treason of the clerks.

Just how widely tempting is the doctrine of social adaptation may be illustrated from the views of one of the most distinguished of contemporary academics. After a decade in which he had been responsible for setting in motion a vast increase in the availability of university places, Lord Robbins has argued as follows:

> In this age, in which it has been decided that university education shall be provided for widening numbers of the relevant age groups, it must be realized that the high proportion of those admitted who are likely to become dons or high experts is becoming less and less and the proportion of those who proceed to less specialized functions more and more. If this is so, then surely it is important that our first degree courses should be arranged so as to meet the requirements of the former—the requirements of the many who do the ordinary work of the world—equally with those of the few who are privileged to pursue rarer tasks.[8]

Lord Robbins has here put his finger on a conspicuous and apparently irrational feature of academic education: that a university degree is technically a licence to teach, and yet most of its graduates will never pick up a piece of chalk in their lives. Is it not obvious that much of the training given in universities is therefore anachronistic and of little relevance to subsequent careers? Yet to press this point is once more to be deluded by a false analogy. If we are constructing a tool, then the more exactly it suits its specific task the better. Nor need this kind of thinking always exclude human

[8] Chancellorship Address, University of Stirling, April 1968.

beings. For example, it has been persuasively argued[9] that many professional men in underdeveloped countries are excessively educated. In tropical countries, medical auxiliaries with standard technical skills could save many lives which are now lost because doctors spend years of an academic training in medicine learning much that they will never need. This is a perfectly sensible opinion which is equivalent to saying that there are many practical problems which it is absurd to solve by academic devices. But it is absolutely fundamental to an understanding of universities to recognize that a graduate is not a tool in any sense at all. To be an academically educated man is not merely to have mastered a skill, but to have understood what it is to master such and such a skill. This involves not merely being able to produce a practical effect (where this is relevant), but being able also to give an account of it. It is this apparent indirection which is both the key to the great practical success of universities, and which can also appear in some circumstances to be an irrationality. It is important to note that the students who graduate from universities are not simply doctors, engineers, linguists, etc, but are also potentially *teachers* of these skills. And since, as we have seen, the distinction between teaching and research is academically crude, it follows that university graduates are also potential contributors to and developers of the skills they have mastered. The price which is paid for this extra dimension is that university graduates still have a lot to learn about practice even after they graduate; but the gain is a considerable increase in depth and resourcefulness. A further price paid is that university education takes a long time, and therefore can only be afforded either by rich and prosperous communities or else by communities which (as in medieval times) considered that learning had some special magic which

[9] E.g. by Ivan Illich, in *Celebration of Awareness*, London 1971, and other writings. Illich, of course, wants to generalize his suggestions by 'de-schooling' society altogether.

warranted the making of sacrifices. On the other hand, it is only those of a speculative bent who really benefit greatly from this specifically academic dimension of things: though it might convincingly be argued that a sojourn away from urgencies in a properly academic world would induce a valuable reflectiveness in quite a wide class of people.

The doctrine of social adaptation is generally presented as if it were a new and sudden irruption of reason into the hidebound traditions of the cloister, but this impression is misleading. It is in fact a doctrine centuries old, and would seem to date from about the seventeenth century, when men like Bacon, Comenius and Locke were beginning to challenge the established view of what education consisted in. Their view was that education was a 'preparation for life', a view appropriate to men who were beginning to take seriously the distinction between child and adult. Given the emergence of this odd belief, it became immediately obvious that Latin and Greek, and much of literature and mathematics, were of no real use to most people, and therefore ought to be replaced by more suitable forms of 'preparation'. This kind of argument often reduced those who thought of education differently – as the cultivation of certain sensibilities not universally distributed among men – to the difficult task of trying to exhibit education as useful. Strange and unlikely views (such as that Latin grammar ought to be studied in order to improve our command of the vernacular) were the outcome of a dilemma whose source really lay elsewhere.

It is the switch from 'education' to 'preparation for life' which began to bring education into politics. For preparation depends on what one is preparing for; and the rulers of modern European states, with an eye to the economic and military strength of their realms, soon began to take an interest in the kind of skills they ought to encourage their subjects to acquire. Here, as we have seen, is the seed of those national systems of education which have developed in modern times. In those countries where the cultural tradition has been feeble, or where immensely powerful governments have extinguished it (all totalitarian countries, for example), education has disappeared, along with other aspects of cultural vitality. One of the common signs of this outcome is a concentration upon the technical to the exclusion of the philosophical.

It is one of the striking features of the history of thought about educational adaptation that it has generally been promoted by educated and clever men on behalf of mediocre and poor ones. Before the exponents of the doctrine of social adaptation had available to them such powerful cries as 'privilege' and 'elitism' they argued in terms (which would now be thought patronizing) of the needs of the poor. They identified education in terms of unpopular contingent characteristics such as snobbishness or traditionalism. There is indeed an echo of this feature of the doctrine in Lord Robbins' concern for 'the many who do the ordinary work of the world', and for whom some special provision (which always involves something far short of excellence) should be made. But the paradox is, of course, that those who need such special consideration ought not to be in universities at all. There is not the slightest reason why all tertiary education should be cast in an academic mould.

The protean energy of the doctrine of social adaptation is a clue to one of the standing difficulties of attempting to describe the specific identity of universities. Every account of this identity is cast upon the waters of social belief, only to drown in seas of ambiguity. For it is a feature of words to have connotations, and the following of a chain of connotations can very rapidly transform a formula of identification into something not very far removed from its opposite. We have already seen one case of this, in that the perfectly reasonable account of universities as 'critical institutions' dedicated to 'questioning what we take for granted' has been transposed into such formulae as 'questioning basic assumptions' or criticizing 'the prevailing orthodoxy'. These

H

201

formula can only be described as liturgical, partly because the intervention of thought would be irrelevant to their true significance, and partly because, if taken strictly, they do not make sense. What makes an assumption 'basic'? Where in the academic world does one find anything seriously describable as an orthodoxy? Even in cases of academic tribalism the agreement goes no further than the tribe, and libraries are always there to testify abundantly to the existence of alternative views. What has happened here is that one formula used to specify the academic has been absorbed by the supportive rhetoric of a political movement.

Similarly, it is possible to give an account of universities either as 'conservative' or as 'revolutionary' institutions. Universities obviously derive a great deal from the past, they are in a special sense the custodians of records, and it is an important part of their trust not to be seduced by mere novelty. On the other hand, these very features often make them the repositories of material which, in the practical world, can come to have subversive and unsettling effects. Both views are mere approximations, and in both cases the terms 'conservative' and 'revolutionary' must be understood as having different meanings from those they have in practical politics. This does not prevent conservatives and revolutionaries, indeed adherents of all political beliefs, from clutching the university in the clammy embrace of attempted ideological alliance.

Again it was often the case in the past that universities described themselves as communities of scholars; and they were indeed communities of men *equally* engaged in some single enterprise: that of pursuing truth and valuing exactness of understanding. This kind of equality however was never for a moment thought to obscure the fact that some members of the community were very much more clever, or more thoughtful, or more widely read than others, and indeed the communal character of universities was precisely constituted by a spontaneous recognition of these very inequalities. A certain degree of intellectual humility, in other words, has always been an important element of the academic world, and this humility has often characterized even the most celebrated of academics in their recognition that the newest undergraduate could ask a crucial question, or the dullest dog might have the solution to a long-standing perplexity. Nor did any of these considerations cut across the fact that the university was also, like all communities, an institution requiring government, and that government brings with it distinctions of rank and status. Nothing could more completely exhibit a misunderstanding of this ancient formula than a collection of university students attempting to use it as an instrument for acquiring power in the government of the university.

Other formulae used to specify the academic have fallen upon evil days because of cultural degeneration in the relevant areas of language. The argument I am advancing for academic autonomy often used to be associated with the description of universities as places for the 'disinterested pursuit of truth'. But what is left of this formula once the word 'disinterested' comes to be carelessly employed (as it mostly is in journalism and conversation) as equivalent to 'uninterested'? Again, the great achievement of universities used to be thought to be the cultivation of 'discrimination', but this word ceases to be a useful specification once it comes to indicate a practical attitude towards different races and colours. Finally, what of the word 'education' itself? It once stood for a human activity of eliciting certain latent intellectual sensibilities by bringing the young into contact with models of beauty and inquiry. But coming in the seventeenth century to embrace all forms of 'preparation for life' it has sunk to signifying the inculcation of any form of useful information. Advice on the dangers of lung cancer has now been elevated to the status of 'health education', while governments announce campaigns in 'traffic education', designed to cut down road accidents. But lest gloom at the onset of barbarism threatens to overtake us, we need to remember Professor A. N. Prior's comparing the task of philosophy to weeding or shaving, etc. Gardens would be less vital without weeds, but on the other hand they disappear altogether if they return to the wild.

10 The Doctrine of Social Transformation

The university is besieged not merely by those who seek to invest it and adapt it to new purposes, but also by those who seek to destroy it altogether. Whereas in earlier times this latter impulse might fleetingly appear in the guise of attacks upon the 'vanity of learning', and later it might camouflage itself in the sheep's clothing of the doctrine of social adaptation, it has now appeared in its full character as the demand for 'de-schooling society'. 'Schools' are here represented as moral enclaves in which the young are processed for a passive acceptance of the injustices of the society in which they will later live. Educational theory has recently become a fertile soil for a form of belief which, for all its apparent affinities with the doctrine of social adaptation, is in fact quite different in quality. Since this belief lacks a full definitive statement, we shall have to stitch together its strands from a variety of hints and indirections. We may call it the doctrine of social transformation and it begins to appear once education has been yoked to politics and construed as an instrument in a fundamental struggle. We may glimpse it briefly when we find David Page writing:

> I don't regard 'Higher Education for All' as an ultimate aim. I hope we look forward to a society which will not draw a line between 'work' and 'education'—in which, indeed, 'work', 'life'

205

(as its antithesis) and 'education' have become meaningless distinctions. But the interim need is for a fully educated society, which would be in itself radically different from ours.[1]

There are many intellectual fields in which this doctrine is being adumbrated, but none in which its full character has been thoroughly explored. Even a superficial consideration, however, will allow us to display certain of the necessary conditions of the academic world.

The fundamental tenet of the doctrine of social transformation is that all barriers between human beings must be destroyed. As with most doctrines, its source can be found in a common human mood, and for an expression of this mood we cannot do better than quote the young Engels. He observed early in life that pedestrians on the streets of London (one of Capitalism's cities of the plain)

. . . crowd by one another as though they had nothing in common, nothing to do with one another, and as if their only agreement were the tacit one that each shall keep to his own side of the pavement, in order not to delay the opposing streams of the crowd, while it never occurs to anyone to honour his fellow with so much as a glance. The brutal indifference, the unfeeling isolation of each in his private interest becomes the more repellent and offensive, the more these individuals are herded together within a limited space.[2]

Here is a mood whose practical outcome is a hatred of the privacy involved in a condition of fellow-citizenship, and an urge to transform society into a band of brothers. The much-quoted phrase from John Donne's sermon, to the effect that no man is an island, owes its modern currency to its appearance of stating this mood. And the fact that the view may be found stated in sermons is a clue to what seems to me to be the most important point about the doctrine of social transformation: namely, that although it generally stalks the world in political forms and hides behind rejections of this or

[1] Rubinstein and Stoneman, *op. cit.*, pp. 214–15.
[2] Quoted in Edmund Wilson, *To the Finland Station*, London 1940, II, 7.

that injustice, it is fundamentally a religious, not a political, doctrine. For as Rousseau remarked at the beginning of *The Social Contract* (and Rousseau at various times shared the mood), government is concerned with 'men as they are, and rules as they might be'. Once a doctrine begins to concern itself with men as they are *not*, it has moved out of the field of politics altogether. The kingdom of heaven, and the post-revolutionary society, in both of which brotherly love will reign, are both expressly conditions far beyond politics.

Possibly for this very reason, one of the first appearances of the doctrine of social transformation was in attacks upon the barrier between ruler and ruled. For to issue a command with authority is to interpose a barrier between oneself and those who have been commanded. Therefore one tactic commonly employed has been to attack the idea of authority as an imposture, and to attempt to replace it with reason, which all men share, and which therefore cannot in principle become a source of barriers. Paine, for example, was merely one of the liveliest of many writers, particularly in England and France, who expressed a hatred for 'the general and mysterious word *Government*'.[3] He regarded its origins as indefensible, its power as unnecessary and its effects as uniformly pernicious. He saw in the Revolutions of America and France the beginning of an irresistible movement which would sweep governments away and replace them by peaceable national associations of men doing cooperatively for themselves what had previously been done by monarchs and aristocrats, and doing it much more cheaply to boot. Many anarchists have shared his views. The philosophical issues involved here are too complicated to come within our compass. But it should perhaps be explained that the notion of authority has generally been defended as deriving from the fact that in politics reason never generates an unequivocal policy. If a government has money to spend, or a problem of foreign policy to solve, there are no doubt many things which would be almost universally thought 'irrational' but there

[3] Thomas Paine, *The Rights of Man*, Part II, Everyman edition, p. 154.

remain a great number of possibilities which appeal power-fully to different sides, and this is a plurality which cannot be reduced to a unity by any process of reason. Men, being passionate creatures, are liable to fight and destroy one an-other unless they institute officers having the authority to end disputes by making a decision which must be accepted. Indeed, even when there *are* such officers, men are still at times liable to fall to fighting. If this is a true account of the human situation, then it would be absurd to regard reason and authority as competing and antipathetic principles; in-deed, it is only recognizing the appropriateness of authority in many practical affairs which prevents the notion of reason from being hopelessly discredited by the pretences of politicians. To put the matter another way, in politics authority is to such an extent inextinguishable, that even the political leader who claims that his policy is indisputably rational must be seen as claiming reason as the *authority* for his act. But, as we have pointed out, no political act can logically claim the warrant of reason; and therefore the claim to rationality as a basis for authority is, paradoxically, itself irrational. Any reader inclined to regard this point as a piece of mere logic-chopping ought to remind himself that govern-ments claiming reason as the authority of their acts have been extraordinarily ruthless in dealing with opponents. For who could doubt that a man who resists 'Reason' must clearly be counted as much more of a scoundrel than a man who merely resists 'Authority'?

The doctrine of social transformation, then, first appeared as one (but only one) of the moods in which political thinkers sought to replace 'Authority' by 'Reason'. Typically, in terms of social transformation, *all* evils were seen as the *systematic* consequence of government: thus Paine believed that if governments were abolished they would take with them poverty, war, excessive taxation, obsequiousness and 'the foppery of titles'. It is an early and spectacular example of the exculpation of human nature at the expense of social institutions. And that it expressed a powerful mood can be seen not only in the French Revolution's passion for 'fraternity' but also in the development of nationalist doctrines to the effect that the really significant barrier was between *foreign* rulers and their subjects, and in the hopes widely entertained in modern times that democratic rulers would be closer to the people than hereditary rulers. The hatred of this particular barrier came to be built in to the specification of all revolutions. 'In our revolution', Fidel Castro has said, 'between the people and the governing power there is not, nor can there be, contradiction.' It is a brave aspiration, which ought to have emptied the prisons and brought the many Cuban exiles home; but it has not, and it remains mere pretence.

Once this doctrine had been fully established, it became an obvious move to discover other and even more fundamental barriers between human beings. That distinctions of wealth and poverty were a barrier of just this kind had long been held in arguments about justice, but in the nineteenth century various writers, Marx and Engels being much the most prominent, began to argue that it was really social classes that constituted the fundamental barrier between human beings, and that all iniquities, even those of government, derived from this source. The Marxist theory of alienation is a brilliant statement of the doctrine I am concerned with: it distils elements common to writers at many levels of sophistication, and connects them up into a system of barriers. The fundamental distinction is between the treatment of supposed injustices piecemeal, or systematically: for the infallible mark of the doctrine of social transformation is that it construes all evils not as isolated examples of injustice which ought to be remedied, but rather as *symptoms of an evil system*, which must be destroyed.

Once elaborated to this degree, the doctrine of social transformation stood available as a device by which any form of supposed injustice might be seen as fundamental.

209

Barriers between races and nations have often been used to explain the scourge of war. That the biological distinction between male and female had developed into a social distinction between masculine and feminine meant a barrier bringing with it injustice to at least one side. Sexual distinctions had led to a barrier between the sexually normal and the homosexual. Even the family divided the human race into small, and for many purposes competing, units : to have brothers stood in the way of human brotherhood. The 'shabby intimacies' (as they have been described) of family life have been seen as forms of oppression. Even sexual fidelity might be interpreted as an exclusiveness liable to disrupt the harmony of the human species. It is clear that the doctrine of social transformation is a theoretical engine capable of developing any human distinction into the fundamental source of all the ills which beset mankind. And although no exponent of this doctrine has been theoretically intrepid enough to follow it through, there can be little doubt of the logical terminus of the doctrine: a single condition of humanity in which no person may be meaningfully specified as distinct from any other person, since to call a human being male or female, gentile or Jew, young or old, black or white, ruler or ruled, would be to invoke one of the barriers. Furthermore, what is held objectionable about the barriers is that the moment they appear they bring with them some element of evaluation likely to induce misery in the excluded or inferior side, and a corresponding distortion of reality even to those who appear to benefit.

The attack on schools and universities is based upon one particular barrier which has long attracted the attention of exponents of the doctrine of social transformation. 'Division of labour', Marx and Engels wrote in an early work, 'only becomes truly such from the moment when a division of material and mental labour appears.'[4] The very emblem of the estrangement of man from man was to be found in the distinction between the educated man and those who per-

[4] R. Pascal (ed.), *The German Ideology*, parts I and III, London 1938, p. 20.

formed merely mechanical tasks. The significance of words like 'privilege' and 'elite' is to indicate that schools are themselves graded in terms of prestige, and that they have the effect of grading children permanently into alphas and betas. By a similar argument, so long as universities are not attended by everyone they will be the generators of a divisive social caste. 'Selection implies losers as well as winners and, increasingly, selection is for life'⁵ writes one exponent of this view, a writer who is in no doubt that the most objectionable feature of barriers is the possibility of winning and losing. For losers resent winners, and winners are encouraged to feel themselves superior to the rest: the ideal fraternal unity of the human species is thus disrupted by something remarkably like the fall of man. It is hard not to see the core of this doctrine as another assault upon man's disposition towards pride. The moment a distinction is allowed to come into existence, it becomes a distinction of value. Some human beings are sold cheap like remaindered books, and they resent it; suffering enters the world. And suffering causes conflict, and thus further suffering. The doctrine of social transformation is the search for a way of reversing this chain of social consequences. If the reversal could ever be achieved, the human race would be compassionately at one, even though made up of physically separate atoms. Men would not suffer, as they do today, from inexplicable barriers to communication, and human life would be the continuous unfolding of creative human spontaneity.

The characterization of this doctrine as religious may well be found implausible by readers who regard religion as essentially concerned with God and an afterlife. To some extent we have met this objection in an earlier chapter, but it is worth rehearsing the curious distortion in eighteenth-century intellectual history whereby attacks upon the specific religion of Christianity found it expedient to present themselves as attacks by Science, Reason or Philosophy upon Religion in general rather than upon one specific religious

⁵ Everett Reiner, *School is Dead*, London 1971, p. 28.

establishment. The rhetorical weapons forged at this time have proved so powerful that most subsequent critics of Christianity have been loath to abandon them, with the result that conspicuously religious passions are to be found representing themselves in political and intellectual terms. The distinction between religion, which we may take to be an understanding of the human situation and the duties appropriate to it, and politics, which we may take to be the activity whereby men make decisions about the rules governing their communal lives, has never been very sharp in practice, but has now become one of the radically unfocused aspects of our civilization. Different considerations are appropriate to each, and in much modern discourse one may observe the mood of the writing switching back and forth between the two. Such blurring is particularly evident in the case of the doctrine of social transformation, for expressions of it are often on the surface concerned with this or that social injustice, educational inefficiency, moral absurdity or political cause. The transition from politics to religion is, as we have said, often to be detected in the treatment of any of these things as symptons of some greater scheme: the people involved in particular cases fade as human beings making choices, into fragments or puppets 'conditioned' by the system of which they are thought to be essentially a part.

The modern idea of revolution in most cases looks remarkably like a political transposition of the religious promise that the meek shall inherit the earth. But the argument that social transformation is a religious rather than a political movement is very much stronger than any conclusions we might draw merely from appreciating the many analogies between this species of apparent politics on the one hand and theological notions on the other. It is clear that the doctrine of social transformation is not about mutual accommodation (which is all that politics can achieve) but about universal love, which would indeed require nothing less than a transformation of human nature as we know it. And like any religion, it generates appropriate hymns:

It was on a Friday morning
They took me from my cell
And I saw they had a carpenter
To crucify as well.

You can blame it on to Pilate
You can blame it on the Jews
You can blame it on the Devil
It's God that I accuse.

It's God they ought to crucify
Instead of you and me
I said to the carpenter
A-hanging on the tree.[6]

This strand of thought suggests very strongly that the doctrine we are concerned with is a new version of a very old religious belief to the effect that the world is the creation of the devil, and that it is the business of the believer to free himself from its shackles. The words of a Bob Dylan lyric use the ancient imagery of the Orphics,

Sometimes I think this whole world is one big prison yard
Some of us are prisoners, the rest of us are guards. . . .

It is a further difficulty of understanding this doctrine that it appeals to intellectual values in order to destroy intellectuality, and individual values in order to destroy individuality. The reason for this is that the vocabulary which allows it to present itself as a form of enlightened higher morality rather than as a competing religion is derived from the academic world. The key terms seem to be 'system' and 'society', but they are supplemented by extensive borrowing from the technicalities of the social sciences, all linked to the moral vocabulary of liberalism. The element of paradox can most easily be seen if we observe the way in which 'liberation' appears to mean the active bringing of 'liberty' but is in fact almost diametrically opposed to it. The argument is that to transform the social system

[6] From a hymn book used in a number of schools, called *New Life* and published in Norfolk. Protests against its use were widely reported in the press in April 1972.

would vastly increase our liberty. For, it is said, each of us is restricted by our private family understandings, class attitudes, sexual roles and so on. If these were removed then we would at last be able to express our individuality without any of the repression which each role imposes. The mistake here is to believe that human individuality is merely a succession of impulses; it consists, rather, in the evolving of settled dispositions and interests which necessarily have the power to repress contrary impulses. If they had not, no impulse could develop beyond a spasm without being rapidly succeeded by another. Further, unless each human being were thought to have identical impulses to every other, those sharing particular interests would begin to cultivate them cooperatively, which would involve exclusion of those not sharing the same interests. To be *at liberty* to develop these dispositions is, then, directly contrary to *the state of liberation* of a transformed society: the state of liberation excludes the possibility of alternatives. The same point may be exemplified by noting that Women's Liberation seeks to abolish the role of housewife as one of the alternatives a woman might choose, whereas in a society concerned with liberty (rather than liberation) such alternatives as house or career would not be foreclosed. The paradox of liberation is its underside of compulsion.

What we have called the doctrine of social transformation is an ideal limit serving to identify the tendency of many strands and wisps of belief currently circulating in the modern world. They may be found in most spheres of life, and they are expressed both in sophisticated and in simple terms. It should be clear that this doctrine is consistently destructive of the academic world, and that if it were to be widely embraced in a religious spirit, universities would disappear. Most totalitarian states are orchestrated to a (generally weakened) politico-religious version of the doctrine, and great efforts are made to prevent the emergence of anything seriously academic. Part of the point of the Cultural Revolution in China in the early 1960s seems to have been to correct professors who 'did not see society as a factory and kept divorcing the students from the masses'. Futan University in Shanghai, one gathers, 'has completely dropped the traditional courses in literature and science and replaced them with such subjects as electronics and optics – and it conducts those classes in its own factories'.[7] There is plenty of evidence that what theory suggests has been heeded in practice. And this allows us to recognize certain important incompatibilities between universities and some features of state and society.

The argument of this chapter and its predecessor has revealed a steady increase in the extent to which education may become the servant of moral and political opinion. From the first faint flutterings of the doctrine of social adaptation, identical to the moment when education was taken to be a 'preparation for life', men of opinion became increasingly bold in seeking to reorganize education to fit what they imagined to be social needs. And in time this bringing of education from the obscure periphery to the lively centre of political preoccupations rendered it vulnerable to the most visionary of social projects: the doctrine of social transformation. The consequent extinction of anything genuinely educational may be seen both in the conclusions of our argument and in the practices of totalitarian governments. It is significant that in totalitarian countries the full weight of the revolution must be brought to bear upon what is recognized as the spontaneous tendency of universities to draw away from practice. Thus the purpose of the regime established at Futan 'university' was stated by its head to be 'to change the situation that prevailed before the Cultural Revolution, when practical knowledge was divorced from theoretical knowledge'. But such assaults upon the academic are not confined to the melodramas of totalitarianism. They include also those occasions when an appeal is made to the university's sense of virtue, occasions when it is exhorted to become an agency for the correction of social injustice. Thus

[7] *Time*, 27 March 1972, p. 44.

universities have often prospered in the past even though such classes of people as blacks, Jews, nonconformists in religion, and women were legally excluded. This exclusion was never on serious academic grounds, and we need not doubt that the university is enriched by the openness of access which has been currently embraced. But this accessibility is entirely distinct from the thoroughly political doctrine that the sociological composition of universities ought ideally to mirror that of society at large, and that where this does not happen it ought to be deliberately brought about. The notion of some divinely pre-established harmony between academic passion and talent on the one hand, and *any* sociological mapping of a society is an evident postulate of the faith required for social transformation. What it would seem in practice to signify is an attempt to fill the universities with as many unsuitable people as possible. The effect of this is to create a political Trojan Horse, since most students admitted on non-academic grounds are easily recruited in support of projects of social adaptation.

It is tempting to try and state the necessary social conditions of the maintenance of the academic world, and indeed our argument has already suggested one important condition: the absence of despotism. For any society in which the writ of a powerful centre suffers no limit at all is a society in which every institution (and not merely universities) has become subservient. It is difficult to conceive of a society in which such a specification would be entirely true, but the twentieth century has presented plenty of attempts to create a comprehensive harmony. Further, since the transformation of society which we have discussed in this chapter would run counter to the irresistible tendency of human beings to cooperate together and thus create institutions independent of and conflicting with the rest of society, it could only be sustained by the continuous application of a powerful despotic pressure which neutralized every appearance of independence. Such a regime would be logically incompatible with academic independence.

But to state a logical incompatibility of this kind is not to state a social condition. Our discussion of the doctrine of social transformation has failed to throw up any very definite social conditions which we could confidently link with universities. Nor is this surprising. Universities have only been invented once; hence there is no material for a general theory of their emergence; and once established they have thrived in many soils, suggesting that we should look to the hardiness of the plant rather than to the suitability of the soil. It is not even the case that they require anything that an Anglo-Saxon liberal would recognize as 'a free society' in which to thrive. This rather negative conclusion is not, however, a disappointment, but a clue to the fact that to look for social factors means that we have asked the wrong question.

For the question: what are the minimum social conditions of universities? assumes that there are some specifiable social conditions which will cause universities to arise and to prosper. But this is to take it for granted that universities are passive and reactive institutions dependent upon the society in which they live. Just such an assumption underlies a vast amount of thinking about the subject. But the fact is that the cultivation of the academic world is itself an independent social condition which will in many circumstances find its own modes of support, just so long as it remains vigorous enough to do so. And vigour is not a function of money or materials so much as a moral circumstance created by self-understanding and a dedication to academic pursuits. There is no reason, of course, to regard an academic tradition as either immortal or indestructible. One might easily imagine a society in which the rewards of power were sufficiently glittering to cause most or all men of talent to desert the calling of inquiry; alternatively a grand catastrophe might easily force whole generations of men back into the urgencies of practice. But once the tradition is established its memory is hard to erase. All that universities require is a society in which it is possible for men to set up independent institutions. This means that both institutions and individuals must be able to gather together some material resources and to dispose of them, from generation to generation, as they see fit, and irrespective of the views either of a government or indeed of the rest of the population. An alternative manner of specifying this general condition is to say that universities require a society in which there is more than one centre of initiative. In such a society, they will often have the support of other independent institutions, such as churches, trade unions, clubs, etc – everything, that is, which has managed to escape the cage called a 'national system'. Such a society is necessarily one in which conflict, inequality and injustice are constantly arising, and just as constantly being politically accommodated. But the dream, nurtured in moods of social transformation, that this imperfect condition of things will ever be replaced by a final harmony is equivalent to the servile preference for peace and security over the perils and fascinations of academic inquiry.

For this reason also, academic independence cannot be subject to any set of universal political rights. There can no more be a universal 'right' to go to a university than there can be a natural right to a PhD, or to take communion, or to enter a private house, or to join a trade union, or any other activity that requires cooperation on the part of the participants. Aristotle once posed the problem of how to distribute a scarce supply of flutes, and came to the unsurprising conclusion that they should be given to the best flute players. In a rich modern society, with an abundance of flutes, it is no doubt possible, and may well be harmless, to give everyone a flute. But to the musically incompetent and the tone-deaf these instruments will be no more than useless lumber. It might well be tempting to apply the same reasoning to universities, but this would be a mistake. For a university (unlike a flute) must have the cooperation of those who participate in its activities; and the mulish, the discontented and the untalented constitute an active weight upon its progress.

We may conclude that the academic world, whose resilience is something of a miracle, and whose appearance is more rare than we commonly realize, will be but a fugitive moment unless the institution of the university is sustained by a plural society in which it may link its independence with the independence of other social institutions, all with material resources to dispose of, within the framework of a rule of law which is not immediately responsive to outside pressure.

11 The Secret University

To conclude: the true identity of universities is buried deep under an accumulated lumber of moral pictics, political doctrines, misleading legends about the past, and irrelevant aspirations towards changing the whole character of human existence. The place of universities in society has become a public question, and as befits a public question it has fallen into the hands of publicists keen to appropriate a valuable resource to the purposes of their commonplace commitments. Once this lumber has been removed, however, the academic world appears as a vast imaginative realm whose range is immensely greater than anything to be found amongst the shifts and schemes of the practical world, because (unlike the practical world) it is not tied down to the limitations of action. The academic mind adventures wherever human experience has led, and passes beyond that experience by its re-creation of lost human pasts or its conjectural probing beyond the range of the telescope or the microscope. It is something which only the rich and the intrepid can afford, for when it hears the voice of its duty to, for example, an underdeveloped country, it can recognize both the virtue of the plea and the academic irrelevance of what is being said. 'The real problem', President Nyerere told an academic audience in June 1966, 'is that of promoting, strengthening and channelling, social attitudes which are conducive to the progress of our society.'[1] But the academics in his audience would have ignored the practical business of 'strengthening' in favour of pressing upon the thin ice revealed by such an idea as 'the social attitudes which conduce to the progress of our society'. If the lives of most people take place within the warm circles of practice, the academic world is to be found flying off at a tangent – a situation it shares with art and lunacy. But a tangent is a lonely place, and therefore an adherence to academic inquiry is often a matter of internal struggle for dons, who are constantly drawn back to the warm circles of practice, and who cannot help experiencing the itch for action.

It is generally some sense of urgency which brings us back into practice, and it is always the voice of urgency which tempts us to see universities as parts of 'Society' (and having a duty to contribute to it) rather than as independent institutions cutting across its grain. Few are the academics so completely absorbed in their work as to be immune to those bold pronouncements by which practical men explain to us our duty in terms of the function, role, purpose or true character of the university. And as we have seen, even quite perceptive accounts of the concept of a university may come to be twisted in this direction. For example, academics are, from one point of view, part of a much larger class of intellectual men (teachers, writers, professional men, and so on) from whom in the public eye they are often barely distinguishable. All such intellectuals are participants in (and often cannibals of) 'culture'. They keep in a state of effervescence that stock of ideas and artistic creations with which mankind has responded to the human situation. This stock is often taken to be the product of a mental faculty called 'the intellect'. It is tempting to explain the university in terms of this cultural entity; thus Lord Annan has written:

The intellect. *That* is what universities are for. Everything else

[1] Julius Nyerere, *Freedom and Socialism*, Dar es Salaam 1968, p. 184

is secondary. Equality of opportunity to come to the university is secondary. The need to mix classes, nationalities and races together is secondary. The agonies and gaieties of student life are secondary. So are the rules, customs, pay, and promotion of the academic staff and their debates on changing the curricula or procuring facilities for research. Even the awakening of a sense of beauty, or the life-giving shock of new experience or the pursuit of goodness itself—all these are secondary to the cultivation, training and exercise of the intellect.[2]

There is obviously much to be said for this view; but time's whirligig has a way of turning sound approximations into dangerous half-truths. The argument of this book, especially its second part, has been that it is important to distinguish the academic from the intellectual. For the university is distant from and often hostile to much of this intellectuality, somewhat as monks to diocesan clergy. Intellectuals are unmistakably inhabitants of the practical world. They quite legitimately embrace causes, conduct vendettas, suppress inconvenient evidence, strike moral postures, succumb to intellectual fashions, scheme, feud and sign petitions. In some countries they constitute an entire social class having great influence on the government. In their care for intellectual matters, the class of intellectuals is a natural ally of universities, but in its practical involvement this alliance can become much more dangerous than open enmity. For it is through this dense protective medium that the blinding enthusiasms of the practical world may try to pass themselves off as ultimate truths which it is the university's duty to diffuse. And it is clear that if the class of intellectuals could ever agree on some set of truths, they would not hesitate to impose it upon universities. Intellectuals are the source of those passionate ideas which periodically seize the imagination of the masses, sometimes even capturing governments, and then demand to be declaimed from the lecture rostrum as final truths.

---

[2] *Encounter*, April 1963; and quoted in an article Lord Annan wrote in the *Times Literary Supplement* for 30 April 1970.

The only thing that universities ought to do is the only thing they can do: sustain the academic world. It is not the wonders with which they have been associated which constitute the splendour of universities: that splendour derives rather from many things which feature little in the public imagination. Over the centuries Europe has often, wherever it found itself in a blind alley, engaged in a kind of dialogue with its classical past. Parts of Greek and Roman experience have appeared at different times in Western thought as the apex of wisdom, the model of art, the pure expression of the rational spirit, and as a liberation of feelings from convention. These possible resources had been kept available by the educative work of universities, but they could only have been kept vital so long as the academic world as a whole (by contrast with enthusiasts within it) did not itself succumb to *any* of these views, but continued to sustain the classics in all the amplitude of academic scholarship. An even more striking achievement of the last two centuries has been the recovery of the human past by archaeologists and historians: for this required not only the illuminating of dark ages but the active discarding of those legends about the past to which all peoples are passionately attached. It involves treating recovered material not as a stimulus to the imagination, nor as buried treasure, but as evidence out of which could be constructed the lives and experiences of peoples long since forgotten. This is an achievement of the human spirit which it is difficult for practical men not to transform into something more banal. It is, further, one of the respects in which the university has acted, as it were, on behalf of mankind. And it is relevant because it reminds us that, though we commonly recognize that the university, being an international institution, transcends national frontiers, we do not so easily recognize its far more important transcendence of the most elusive and parochial of all provincialisms: that of the present moment.

Once we remove the cluster of philosophical confusions which we discussed in chapter 4 (such as that between expert and academic, for example, or between a hypothesis and a justification), it becomes clear that academics are the cultivators of a secret. This is not at all to suggest that they deliberately traffic in secrets; indeed, the great strength of universities (by contrast with forms of enlightenment found in other civilizations) has been their steadfast refusal to turn understanding into a kind of vulgar esotericism. On the contrary, they have always insisted that the body of knowledge they cultivate is in principle open to anyone who is prepared to give the time and the wits to it. It is merely a contingent feature of the world (but a contingency never likely to disappear) that most men have not the interest or the time to follow the scholar into this world. To act is necessarily to embrace a kind of passionate blindness, and most men most of the time are more concerned to act and react rather than to understand. Journalism, popularization and ideology are there in abundance to testify to what happens to academic inquiry as it crosses the invisible boundary into the practical world. Endless disputes between theologians and scientists, more recently between politically divided psychologists and biologists on the subject of race and intelligence, testify to the many pressures, particularly those of human anxiety, which transform hypothetical propositions into saving or damning truths. And even among the widely educated classes of a developed modern society, the sense of the hypothetical attitude sustained by the academic world mostly appears as a kind of dogma about free inquiry and unfettered discussion.

It is difficult to present the argument of this book without seeming to adopt two highly misleading attitudes. The first of these results from the fact that the practical world is an inferior place to the academic. For as it presses upon the academic, it necessarily appears as a vulgarization. Hence, when universities are not being attacked for lack of adaptation, they are being flattered for the integrity of their values and the gossamer fineness of their reasoning. The common argument which places the university at the centre of culture

224

and civilization attributes to it a greater fineness and intelligence than is found outside. On occasions this may well be so, but it is certainly no part of the identity of the academic. For much academic work (like any kind of work) is dull under-labouring requiring no very elevated talent for achievement. By contrast, the practical world includes the marvels of technology and social organization which exhibit intelligence on a scale seldom or never seen in universities. It is often true, of course, that these marvels could not have been produced without the fruits of academic inquiry; but it is also true that they require much else, and that the university unaided could not have created them.

The other misunderstanding is likely to be that the argument of this book amounts to the recommendation of some possibly desirable but hopelessly remote ideal. The constantly dismissive use of the phrase 'ivory tower'[3] (generally coupled with an insistence on the university's links with society) exemplifies the common practical view of universities. Hence it is necessary to emphasize that all over the world, in many universities, exactly the kind of work I have been describing is in fact going on in most of the subjects studied. It is true, of course, that much else is also happening: work on outside contracts, intrigue, careerism and the setting up of merely fashionable courses and subjects of research. It is also true that many undergraduates at universities have no very clear idea of what they are doing, and acquire nothing more sophisticated than the mastery of a few useful skills. This is merely to say that if the argument of this book pretended to be a sociology of modern university practices, it would have to be dismissed as wrong. But it is not; it is rather an attempt at the philosophical exercise of describing the identity which makes universities distinct from other organs of instruction. Even if it were true, which it is not, that no one today could be found cultivating the acad-

---

[3] For an excellent account of the history of this expression, see Professor C. V. Bock's inaugural lecture *The Ivory Tower*, published by Westfield College, London 1970.

emic world, the conclusions of this argument would not, by that fact alone, be invalidated.

In the day-to-day life of universities, then, practical and academic tendencies jostle and conflict with one another, and we need not regret that this is so. For it is often by entering into conflict with things that we understand ourselves best. The tangent would merely be a line without the circle.

To argue for a distinction which most people cannot recognize cuts against the grain of a time when most people do not hesitate to take the limits of their own wits for the contours of what there is. These people have available the use of that agreeable reductionist story by Hans Christian Andersen in which the little child refuses to be taken in by the rascally tailors and leads the crowd in shouting that the Emperor has no clothes on. That story has for the moment done its work, and perhaps a little more. It needs to be re-written to take account of new dangers: in fact the tailors were men of great wisdom and insight who had woven themes too subtle for the populace to follow. The Emperor and his ministers were perfectly right to respect what they did not understand, and the small child who pointed to the Emperor's nakedness was an embryonic demagogue encouraging the populace to be dogmatic about its own blindness.

Index

227

Index

229

Index

Rashdall, Hastings, 11, 12, 27, 31
rationalist, 32, 55
rationality, 1, 67, 72
Regnum, 13
Reiner, Everett, 211n
religion, 32, 34, 35, 36, 37, 38
religion, Roman, 32
renaissance, 12th Century, 13, 22
research, 71
Ricardo, David, 176
Robbins, Lord, 198
Robbins Report, 54, 193
Robespierre, 44
Robinson, Eric, 54n
Roman Law, 14
Roman politics, 33
Romulus, 33
Rosen, Sumner, 176
Roszak, Theodore, 167n, 168n, 176n
Rothblatt, Sheldon, 37n
Rousseau, Jean Jacques, 207
Rubenstein, David, 164n, 190n, 195n, 206n
Russell, Bertrand, 131, 179

Sacerdotium, 13
Saint-Simon, 26
Scholasticism, 18, 63
science, 32, 68, 92, 93, 128
'scientism', 176
Seeley, J. R., 37n
Seminaries, 26
Shakespeare, William, 138
Shils, Edward, 171, 172
Surkin, Marvin, 163n, 167n, 169n, 171n
Social Adaptation, Doctrine of, 187–204
socialization, 6
social sciences, 60
Social Transformation, Doctrine of, 205
Socrates, 16, 32, 70, 107
Stalin, Joseph, 51, 112
Stoneman, Colin, 164n, 190n, 195n, 206n
Storre, Margaret, 27

Strauss, Leo, 46n
studium generale, 11, 12, 13, 62
studium particulare, 62
suicide, 38
Swift, Jonathan, 88

technical schools, 6, 26
technology, 25, 26, 92
Teilhard de Chardin, Pierre, 131
textbooks, 117, 134
Thales, 1
Theodosius, 41
theologia, 15
Thueydides, 52
Time, 215n
Times, 117, 125, 129
Times Literary Supplement, 115, 222
Tomalin, Nicholas, 133
Toryism, 109, 110
totalitarian states, 48
Toynbee, Arnold, 137
Trotsky, Leon, 147
Tucker, Robert, 147

undergraduates, 69–72, 134–5
understanding, 39
universities, 12; attacks on, 27, 54, 55, 185; decadence of, 27, 62–6, 195; distinction of, 57–8; independence of, 61, 101; interpretation of, 26; medieval, 3, 12, 15, 20, 24, 62; modern, 1, 196; relevance of, 27, 163; rise of, 22, 23, 24; vitality of, 52, 67, 99
University Grants Committee, 54, 191
urgency, 98
Usher, Archbishop, 36

value judgement, 88, 96, 143, 144
Vebleu, Thorsten, 2
Virgil, 192
vocational training, 2, 53
voting, 108, 126

Weber, Max, 45

230